Bad Golf
My Way

Bad Golf
My Way

by

Leslie Nielsen
and Henry Beard

Photography by E. H. Wallop

Produced by Patty Brown

A JOHN BOSWELL ASSOCIATES BOOK

DOUBLEDAY
NEW YORK LONDON TORONTO SYDNEY AUCKLAND

PUBLISHED BY DOUBLEDAY
a division of Bantam Doubleday Dell Publishing Group, Inc.
1540 Broadway, New York, New York 10036

DOUBLEDAY and the portrayal of an anchor with a dolphin are trademarks of
Doubleday, a division of Bantam Doubleday Dell Publishing Group, Inc.

Library of Congress Cataloging-in-Publication Data
Nielsen, Leslie, 1925–
        Bad golf my way / Leslie Nielsen and Henry Beard
            p. cm.
        1. Golf--Humor.   I. Beard, Henry.   II. Title.
        GV967.N46   1996
        796.352'0207--dc20   96-33728
                                          CIP

Design by Barbara Cohen Aronica
Typesetting by Jackson Typesetting Company

Photograph appearing on page 6 copyright © 1996 Dennis Kunkel,
University of Hawaii.

ISBN: 0-385-48351-1

To the unknown inventor of the game of golf
who long ago in a distant land beside a savage sea
first hit a small round stone toward a shallow hole with a crooked stick,
and to the huge bear who, if there is any justice in this world,
pounced on him as he stood there studying his shot
and tore him into tiny shreds,
this book is dedicated.

ACKNOWLEDGMENTS

The authors wish to express their gratitude to the following individuals whose assistance in the production of this book is deeply appreciated:

Barbaree Earl, who helped out at the nineteenth hole; Bill Chapman, Leslie's long-suffering opponent; Joel Harris, the chief photographer's assistant; Rich Taylor and Tim Suzor, professionals at the Camelback Inn Golf Club; Stacia Anest in the Camelback Inn Golf Club pro shop; Joyce Palmer of Union Tours in New York City, who handled complex travel arrangements in the middle of the blizzard of '96; Ward Calhoun; and Amy Handy, our dedicated copy editor.

And very special thanks to Sandy Staples and the entire management and staff of Marriott's Camelback Inn in Scottsdale, Arizona.

CONTENTS

Introduction   xi

Chapter   1   Getting Off to a Good Bad Start   1

Chapter   2   Swinging the Club   19

Chapter   3   Making the Bad Golf Shots   33

Chapter   4   Taming the Course   53

Chapter   5   Mastering the Mind Game   79

Chapter   6   Playing to Win   97

Chapter   7   Behaving Well While Playing Badly   121

Suggested Further Reading   129

Recommended Viewing   129

INTRODUCTION

I can't tell you how many times people approach me out on the golf course and say, "Leslie, your two golf videos, *Bad Golf Made Easier* and *Bad Golf My Way*, and your book *Leslie Nielsen's Stupid Little Golf Book*, have utterly transformed my game, not to mention my life, and for this alone you have my undying gratitude. But when, oh when, will you deign to collect all of your bad golf wisdom into a single profusely illustrated, yet attractively priced volume, which I may purchase for my own edification and/or as a thoughtful gift for my playing friends and relatives?" Or words to that effect.

Well, to this enormous handful of avid fans and admirers, and to the thousands of others too shy to express their innermost desires who simply come up and ask me for an autograph, but in whose faces I can read the same feverish yearning for a definitive bad golf instructional manual, I say beseech me no further beseeches. The handsome volume you are now holding in your (recently washed, I trust) hands—*Leslie Nielsen's Bad Golf My Way*—is the book you have been waiting for, and thanks to modern publishing technology, it has been produced so speedily that you may not even have had time to realize that you were waiting for it before it appeared on the shelves of your local bookstore!

And if I may say so, it was worth the wait, even if you were not actually aware that you were in fact waiting for it, because *Leslie Nielsen's Bad Golf My Way* is the first golf text to describe fully the ins and outs of the game that the vast majority of golfers really play and the only one they have any hope of mastering— bad golf.

This is not another useless guide to the alien pastime depicted on TV that is practiced by a few hundred born-lucky professionals with God-given swings, robotlike concentration, and a warped predilection for endless hours of stupefying practice. No, this is a book for the rest of us—the thirty million players whose ingenuity, creativity, and determination have proven over the years to be more than a match for the worst that golf course architects, rule-makers, and teaching pros can throw at them.

As you peruse these pages and absorb the bad golfing secrets and techniques I have developed over a lifetime of deeply uninspired play, I hope you will always remember that golf is meant to be fun, and that you will keep in mind the bad golfer's mantra: "I don't play golf to feel bad—I play bad golf but I feel good." You may also find it helpful in your darkest moments to reflect on the inescapable fact that no matter how badly you are playing, there is almost certainly someone somewhere in the world who is playing worse.

I know what you are going to say. You are going to say, "Leslie, thank you from the bottom of my heart for making this truly extraordinary contribution to my enjoyment and appreciation of truly rotten golf." Well, really, I'm very touched, but I am happy just to give back to golf a little taste of what it has given me over the years, and if I have seen further, it is only because I have stood, in spiked shoes, on the shoulders of giants.

But enough of the preliminaries. Let's tee that sucker up, and plaaaaaaaaay golf!

CHAPTER 1

Getting Off
to a
Good Bad Start

THE BALL

Most golf books start with the grip, or the clubs, or the setup for the swing, and I'm going to get to those in a moment, but I want to begin *Bad Golf My Way* with what I believe to be the single most important element in the game of golf —the ball.

Frankly, the main reason why I can say with confidence, "I don't play golf to feel bad—I play bad golf, but I feel *good*"—is that I discovered long ago one of the few secrets of the game that actually lasts for more than six holes, namely, that you are not playing golf against the course or against an opponent—you are playing against *the ball*.

Make no mistake. That golf ball sitting there so innocently on a tee or a little tuft of grass is your mortal enemy. Left to its own sinister devices, it will go exactly where you don't want it to, and absolutely refuse to go where you do want it to. In fact, it will do anything in its power to thwart your wishes, undermine your confidence, and destroy your composure, because beneath that placid dimpled exterior seethes an inner core of unmitigated animosity for every golfer who ever played the game (Figure 1-1).

Now, at first glance, a golf ball doesn't look like a very formidable adversary. It's small. It stays still while you take a swat at it. You, on the other hand, are large, and you're allowed to move all you want. Not to mention the fact that you have your choice of fourteen heavy clubs to clobber that ball with, and you get to decide exactly when and in what direction to send it flying. Piece of cake, right?

Well, it would be, except for a few minor details. First of all, that wily sphere does have a few natural abilities, like rolling into divots and gullies and footprints in bunkers and other low places where it's hard to get the club on it, and

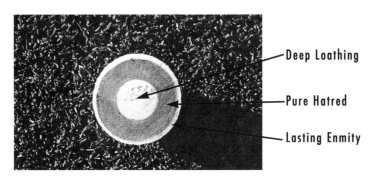

Deep Loathing

Pure Hatred

Lasting Enmity

Figure 1-1. The Face of the Enemy. An ordinary three-piece golf ball.

Figure 1-2. Common Golf Ball Hiding Places. Where's Balldo? There are over 100 balls cleverly concealing themselves in this picture. How many can you spot?

hiding in trees and brush where you can't find it (Figure 1-2), and sinking like a stone in water, usually after two or three tantalizing hops across the surface. And it can do all this while still managing to stop dead in its tracks halfway down a 45-degree slope or on the inner lip of the cup (Figure 1-3).

But a golf ball's most insidious power, ironically, stems from what would seem to be its greatest weakness—it can't move. All it can do is sit there and

Figure 1-3. A Hanging Putt. Hard to believe that sucker didn't sink, isn't it?

stare at you, daring you to hit it. And thus, when you step up there, club in hand, you have all the time in the world to think of one of the slightly more than nine million reasons why you might miss it.

This duel of wits between man and ball puts unimaginable pressure on the one portion of your anatomy least capable of dealing with it—your head (Figure 1-4). And as you bring the club down, your head can do only one thing to relieve this unbearable tension.

It lifts up, of course, so your swing goes blooey, and the ball flies happily away into the trees where, if there is any justice in the world, it will eventually be eaten by a bear.

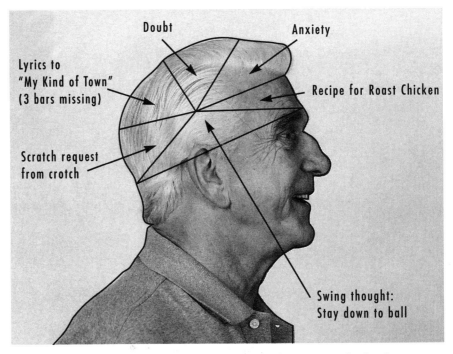

Figure 1-4. The Human Head. (An uncommonly handsome example, by the way!)

Before we go any further, let's take a look at the weapons the bad golfer has at his disposal in this take-no-prisoners battle with the golf ball.

Leaving aside the putter (an excellent idea, if you ask me), all golfers, good and bad, use the same kinds of clubs (Figure 1-5): a few woods, which are usually made out of metal, not wood, and a bunch of irons, which are generally made out of steel, not old frying pans. (Incidentally, I find this things-are-not-what-they-seem aspect of the game of golf one of its great

> ### IS THE PUTTER REALLY A CLUB?
>
> Since the putter is only of real use to a golfer on at most one day out of three or four, many players (myself included) feel it should be classified as an occasional golfing accessory, like a ball retriever, which leaves room in the bag for a "fifteenth" club, maybe an extra wedge or a 9-wood. The fact that many putters can in fact be used as ball retrievers merely underscores the correctness of this interpretation.

charms. There you are, down in the dumps, and suddenly what looked like a score of seven on a particular hole proves, after careful recalculation, to be a five, and a ball that first appeared to be in deep rough behind a tree turns out on closer examination to be sitting up nicely in the fairway.)

The clubs have numbers on their heads that give the pros, with their dull, predictable swings, a good idea of how far they'll hit the ball with that particular wood or iron, but really, for the bad golfer, whose shots are rich in suspense,

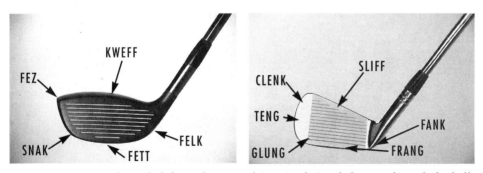

Figure 1-5. A Typical Wood (left) and a Typical Iron (right) and the sounds made by balls hit at various points on the clubface.

WHAT CLUBS ARE BEST FOR YOU?

Professional players have a lot to think about when they pick out a set of clubs, like swing weight and flexpoint and endorsement fees, but for the bad golfer, the primary consideration in buying clubs should always be their appearance. You can go a long way toward making up for an awkward grip and an ugly swing by using good-looking clubs with fancy heads and nifty gold, black, or red graphite shafts.

There is also an intimidation factor at work here, since you can often demoralize an opponent by suggesting that a poor shot he just hit is the result of his using crummy clubs, which is something he clearly can't correct halfway through the round.

On the other hand, if you play with really ratty-looking clubs, other players may suspect you of being a secret sandbagger who's going to suddenly start parring everything in sight somewhere around the eleventh hole, and they might end up questioning your perfectly legitimate 42-handicap.

Figure 1-6. The So-Called Sweet Spot. It's in the center of this photo of the clubface of a 6-iron taken with an electron microscope.

FIGURE 1-7. YARDAGE TABLE

These are about the maximum distances clubs are hit by an average bad golfer.

Club	Yards	Club	Yards	Club	Yards
3-iron	100	Driver	160	Pitching wedge	90
4-iron	125	3-wood	200	Lob or loft wedge	70
5-iron	150	5-wood	200	Sand wedge	175
6-iron	130	7-wood	160		
7-iron	125				
8-iron	100				
9-iron	85				

their main purpose is to let you know which one is missing if you leave a club out on the course.

The actual distance a bad golfer is going to hit a ball with any club obviously depends on many factors, not the least of which is whether the ball was actually hit at all, so it does vary somewhat from shot to shot and player to player, but the table in Figure 1-7 yields a pretty reliable yardage—certainly a lot closer to reality than those charts you see printed in most golf books.

The major difference between the way good and bad golfers strike the ball is that good golfers generally hit the ball with a solid "thwock" in the dead center of the clubface, on the so-called theoretical "sweet spot" (Figure 1-6), while the less skilled player generally uses the entire clubface, as well as the sole, the back, and, occasionally, the shaft of the club to produce the dizzying array of interesting sounds and fascinating flight patterns that are the hallmark of his game.

THE GRIP

In golf, you always hear a lot about the grip, and how important it is for your palms to be parallel, and for the Vs formed by your thumbs and forefingers to be pointed somewhere between your chin and your shoulder, and for two—or is it three?—knuckles of your left hand to be visible, but I think the only really indispensable ingredient in a golf grip is that it must be comfortable.

Think about it. You're going to be using that grip to swing the club more than a hundred times each round, not counting putts (and not counting putts is an excellent idea, I might add), and unless you're a Zen master or some kind of weenie, you're going to be swinging *hard*, because let's face it, most of the fun in golf is whacking the daylights out of the ball.

Now, if you adopt a rigid, exaggerated, or artificial grip some pro talked you into, after a few holes your hands are going to be too stiff and sore to perform the delicate motions that are absolutely essential for a good game of bad golf—motions like the deft tempo-spoiling Velcro tab rip at the top of an opponent's backswing or the light-fingered ball-marking maneuver that shortens a knee-knocking four-foot putt by a hard-to-spot, but crucial, twenty inches.

So go ahead and put your hands on the club any way that feels right to you, just so long as you grip it at the end that has the rubber stuff on it, and not at the end where that curvy metal thing is (Figure 1-8). Which basic style of grip you use—the Vardon, the Interlocking, the Baseball Grip, or some other variation—is really up to you, though there are a few methods that I really don't recommend, except to players who regularly beat me (Figure 1-9). I myself use a variation of the Vardon Grip, probably because when I was taking up the game in my youth, I thought they were saying "Hard-on Grip," and I figured I had that one down pat already.

Figure 1-8. The Basic Grip.

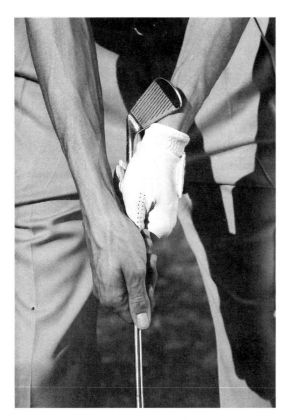

wrong

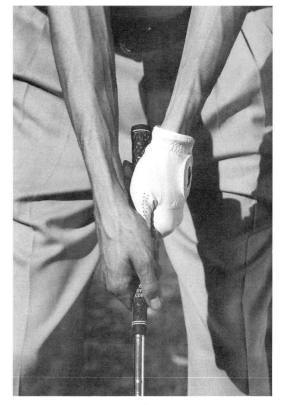

right

GRIP PRESSURE—HOW MUCH IS ENOUGH?

Someone once wrote that you should grip the club as lightly as you would if you were holding a baby bird in your palm, and you were trying to keep it from flying away without crushing it to death. Obviously, this person was a lunatic.

You should hold every club, except possibly the putter, as if it were a poisonous cobra capable of sinking its venom-slathered fangs into your body in one second flat if you relax your grip for even an instant.

To practice this grip—I call it the Darth Vader Death Grip—get a large carrot and boil it for about a minute. Now, grip the carrot just as you would a golf club. Squeeze as tightly as you can. When little squirts of carrot puree start to appear between your fingers, your grip pressure is about right.

Figure 1-9. Grips I Do Not Recommend—Except to Opponents.

Pipefitter

Psycho

Piccolo

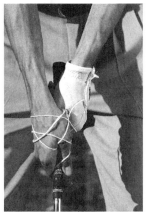

Cat's Cradle

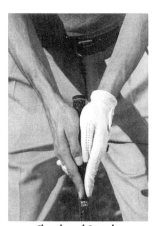

Church and Steeple

Blowgun

Aspen

Look Ma

THE STANCE

I can't tell you how often I've heard people say that the correct way to take your stance when you address the ball is to stick out your butt and deeply flex your knees as if you were executing the first part of the move you'd make to sit down on a barstool. This makes absolutely no sense.

I simply cannot imagine why anyone in his right mind would want to make the first, most uncomfortable and least rewarding move of sitting on a barstool if he weren't going to go ahead and make the rest of the motion (Figure 1-10), including move 2 (resting his behind on the comfy cushion); move 3 (ordering a drink); move 4 (scooping up a handful of peanuts); move 5 (taking a sip of the drink); and move 6 (turning to talk to the attractive young lady on the next bar stool).

Frankly, it seems to me that unless you commit one of a handful of serious but fairly rare stance errors (Figure 1-11), just about any reasonable posture that feels right to you is going to be a whole lot better than standing there like someone who's too dumb to buy beer.

Here's how I position myself to hit the ball. I plant my feet a comfortable distance apart, toes pointed a little out, with the ball right out front and aligned with the fly of my trousers just as if I was about to answer a call of nature in the woods and the ball was a rock or a dandelion I was using as a target.

Naturally, this is a "dry run" so my zipper is in a "closed" position, but I still want the ball close enough so I wouldn't have to lengthen my "arc" unnecessarily, though not so close that I'd hit a "splash" shot. I adopt a wary, watchful stance, without being too jumpy or furtive, and I keep my hands low and centered on my crotch (Figure 1-12).

Figure 1-10. Positioning Yourself for a Highball. An excellent stance for use on the always enjoyable nineteenth hole.

1. Point rear end at stool and begin gentle downward motion.

2. Transfer weight from feet to large muscles of butt.

3. Extend right arm and move hand and fingers back and forth to get bartender's attention and order drink.

4. Cup palm and scoop snack with smooth wrist snap.

5. Bend right elbow sharply to sample drink.

6. Turn hips and shoulders to face neighboring stool.

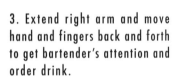

GET SET FOR A GREAT SHOT!

A very useful image to share with an opponent who pays a lot of attention to setting himself into exactly the right stance is to remind him that if a golfer is in the 100 percent absolutely perfect ball-addressing position recommended by all the pros, then a high-velocity bullet fired directly down into the top of his right shoulder would also smash his right elbow, shatter his right kneecap, and blow off the front of his right foot.

Figure 1-11. Rare but Serious Stance Errors. Watch out for these potential shot-wreckers!

1. Too close

2. Too far ahead

3. Too few feet

4. Too many feet

Figure 1-12. My Number 1 Ball-Striking Stance. Notice how my posture at address perfectly blends relaxation and alertness.

Figure 1-13. Poor Ball Position. Take it from me—if you don't pay attention to the all-important "shorts game," you're headed for a world of hurt!

This puts the ball on notice that I am ready for anything it might try to pull (or push or slice), and that if it ends up in the woods after I hit it, the next time I address it I might just take up a more "open" position and give it a real soaking it won't soon forget.

Now as for the correct ball position, well, really, I think that's a personal matter, but here again I really want to emphasize the importance of comfort. (Figure 1-13).

THE SETUP

The way many golfers rush right up and hit the ball with practically no preliminaries makes it look as though they think they can "fool" the ball or "catch it napping" before it gets a chance to mess with their heads.

This is a serious mistake for two reasons. First of all, I can tell you from personal experience that no matter how rapidly or stealthily you approach the ball, you can never succesfully "get the jump on it." It takes only a split second to register its presence in your consciousness, and then it's got you, because once your head knows it's there, it cannot be convinced that it isn't there, even if, say, you cover the ball with a handkerchief because *you must use that very same head to plan and accomplish the task!* (Figure 1-14).

But most important of all, if you just step up and hit your drive with a minimum of fuss and delay, you are forgoing a golden opportunity to drive an opponent nuts. To put it another way, the primary reason you should immediately develop a well-thought-out, multipart, highly repeatable method of approaching the ball, fiddling with your grip, aligning yourself, adjusting your stance, waggling the club, wiggling your hips, and anything else you can think of, is not in the expectation that an extended preshot routine will improve your game in any way whatsoever, but rather in the certain knowledge that it will help immeasurably to destroy an adversary's concentration.

For this reason, I have perfected a procedure for setting up to the ball that, in its most extreme form, requires almost eight minutes to complete (Figure 1-15). Now I am certainly not suggesting that you should try to employ a system anywhere near this complex or time-consuming, but I will say that the best way for a bad golfer to make up for his lack of length off the tee is by the lengths he is willing to go to while he's still on it.

Figure 1-14. "Ball-Fooling" Setups. I've tried them all, and believe me, they don't work.

The Sneak Attack

The Nonchalant Method

The Stealthy Approach

The Camouflage Technique

Figure 1-15. My Preshot Routine. On this page and the next appears just the first part of my classic setup procedure. I'm really sorry there isn't space in a book like this to do it justice.

 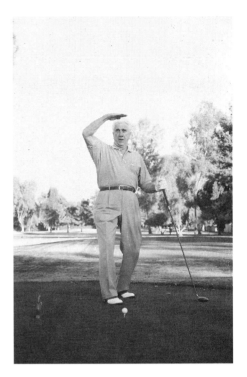

· · · · · · · · · · · · ·

CHAPTER 2

Swinging
the Club

THE RIGHT SWING

The only subject that has had as many words written about it as the golf swing has is sex, and when you think about it, that makes sense, since sex and golf are pretty much the same—with either one, you look silly doing it, the good parts last about six seconds, and it always ends up costing a bundle.

But there is one big difference between the two. Unlike sex (well, unlike *most* sex), the golf swing is a completely unnatural act. In fact, if you believe what they say in golf books, it seems as though the most reliable way to tell that your swing is absolutely correct is for you to be convinced that every single thing you do from the moment you start the club back until you finish your follow-through is 100 percent totally wrong.

Chances are you haven't had that feeling of total wrongness when swinging a golf club since the last time you took a lesson from your local pro, and if you're like me, you're in no hurry to repeat it (Figure 2-1). If that's the case, you've also probably decided, as I have, to pretty much stick with the swing you're stuck with, and make the best of a bad thing, which, when you come right down to it, is the essence of Bad Golf.

So when you ask, "Which swing is right for me?" my answer is simple: it's *the wrong swing*. But, I hasten to add, it has to be the *right* wrong swing, and at all costs you must avoid the ultimate bane of bad golfers everywhere—the dread *wrong* right swing (Figure 2-2).

Now, just because your swing is wrong doesn't mean it has to be ugly. In fact, with surprisingly little effort you can develop a really pretty swing (Figure 2-3). It's also worth keeping in mind one enormous benefit of keeping the swing you already have—there is virtually no need whatsoever to practice it (Figure 2-4).

Figure 2-1. The Lesson Tee. This is potentially the most hazardous spot on any golf course. If in a moment of temporary insanity you succumbed to the urge to improve and scheduled a lesson, you can limit the damage somewhat by pretending to the pro that you're a left-handed golfer (or vice versa).

Remember what I said in the last chapter about the value of a long and complicated preshot routine? Well, that goes double for the practice swing. If you don't make a habit of taking a carefully rehearsed trial cut at the ball *every single time you get up to hit*, then you are missing a golden opportunity to save strokes, not to mention saving face.

Let me make myself clear. As a means of improving your ball-striking, a practice swing is utterly useless, because the rhythmic, effortless, perfectly timed motion you make with a golf club as you swish it over the empty turf bears no relation whatsoever to the urgent, stump-removing hack you're going to employ when you go to hit a golf ball.

But properly performed, a practice swing can provide an iron-clad alibi for a total whiff. That's why I always take my practice swings *directly over the ball*, being careful that the clubhead passes two or three inches above it. I also always make it a point to look as serious and full of concentration as I would if I were actually hitting the ball (Figure 2-5).

If I accidentally *do* catch hold of the ball during this maneuver, as occasionally happens, it's no big deal, because I invariably hit it a mile since I have accomplished by chance what golfers always aspire to but never achieve: I've somehow managed to hit the ball with that lovely, silky smooth, nice-and-easy practice swing.

Figure 2-2. A Truly Scary Sight. Here, at great personal risk, I've taken up a classic wrong right swing. Note the strangely rigid left arm, the horribly folded right elbow, and the terrifying sense of tension. I took the precaution of sedating myself heavily before assuming this awful position, and after the picture was taken, I laid out a hefty sum to a professional hypnotist to remove any traces of the posture from my memory.

THE WAGGLE AND THE FORWARD PRESS

Golfers are often instructed to dispel the tension before they begin their swings with a few back-and-forth "waggles" of the club, followed by a "forward press" motion of the feet, hips, and hands. Since in my view tension is the hidden powerhouse of the golf swing, I want to *increase* it, not reduce it, so I initiate my swing with a "throttle," or slight strangling motion in which I screw my hands tighter on the grip, and a good hard "jaw press," in which I solidly clench my teeth together.

But don't overdo it. The throttle requires only about as much pressure as you would need to choke to death a medium-sized chicken, and the jaw press involves no more force than it would take to bite an ordinary plastic pocket comb in half.

Figure 2-3. The Keys to a Beautiful Swing. With just a little preparation, you can have the nicest-looking swing on the course. A few minutes spent in front of a mirror in the locker room pays big dividends on the first tee.

Figure 2-4. On the Wrong Track. I hate to see a golfer go out to the driving range and hit bucket after bucket in a hopeless attempt to master someone else's swing when he already could do his own in his sleep.

Figure 2-5. A Practice Swing (left) and a Total Whiff (right). Or is it the other way around? I defy anyone to tell the difference.

THE FULL SWING

To get the most out of the golf swing, the bad golfer needs to have a clear picture of the basic physical principles that allow him to smack the ball with such stupendous force.

The most important thing to understand is that although the feet, legs, hips, shoulders, and arms all play a minor role in hitting the ball, the real power in the golf swing comes from the muscles of the neck, which are literally dragged into action by the immense lateral and vertical turning power of the head as it slides sideways at the beginning of the downswing, and then suddenly lifts sharply upward just as the clubhead reaches a point about waist high, when it's still three or four feet from the ball (Figure 2-6).

The momentum generated by the rotary torque of the head is instantly transferred directly to the wrists, which fling the shaft down and forward in a powerful casting motion that sends the clubhead hurtling ahead of the suddenly motionless hands and shifts all of the golfer's weight onto the toes of his front foot.

This instantaneous release of stored-up muscular tension, which is triggered at the top of the backswing by an overwhelming urge to scoop the ball off the ground, is the source of the convulsive upward thrust of the arms and shoulders that gives an observer the unmistakable impression at the moment of impact that the bad golfer has just hefted a large piece of heavy luggage onto an airport conveyor belt.

An indication of the awesome energy unleashed by this colossal upper-body wrench is that if the blow is even slightly misdirected, the club can easily dislodge a slab of sod weighing several pounds, and the sheer inertia generated as the club continues to accelerate after it passes the ball often tears the grip from the golfer's grasp at the end of the swing and pulls one or more of his feet out of his shoes.

Although this series of movements seems quite complicated, it's really the most natural way to swing a golf club, and most bad golfers execute this classic motion completely by instinct. Nevertheless, I'm going to break the Full Bad Golf Swing down into its twelve parts (Figure 2-7)—the Grab, the Snatch, the Lift, the Sway, the Tilt, the Throw, the Lunge, the Heave, the Jerk, the Smasheroonie, the Lurch, and the Recovery—and illustrate each one individually, because even the best bad golfer can make a better bad swing (Figure 2-8).

Figure 2-6. What I See When I Swing. A miniature camera attached to my hat captures the dynamic centrifugal motions of my head that are responsible for the explosive force I create as I crush the ball.

Figure 2-7. The Full Bad Swing in Pictures. The twelve parts of the swing are shown on these two pages. I have omitted the usual tedious blow-by-blow commentary because really I think to fully appreciate the power and grace of my ball-striking action, you need to study it as a whole, preferably while seated in a comfortable chair with a cold beverage within easy reach.

BAD GOLF MY WAY

HOW FAST SHOULD YOU SWING?

Good golfers may be able to hit the ball a ton with an effortless motion that looks like something the rest of us would use to sweep a cat off a couch, but for the bad golfer the secret to getting good distance, particularly off the tee, lies in developing supersonic clubhead speed in the two-thousandths of a second between address and impact.

Basically, I don't think you're swinging too fast unless the wooden tee or a patch of grass near it catches fire, or the ball explodes, or the club hits your left shoulder before you consciously begin your downswing, or you start your backswing while the ball is still in the ballwasher.

Figure 2-8. A *Bad* Bad Swing. While not as bad as a bad *good* swing, this is not one of my better bad swings. I think I was a little late lifting up my head.

SWING FAULTS AND FIXES

Considering the serious damage that can be done to the game of even halfway decent players by a deliberate attempt to change any aspect of the golf swing, no matter how trivial, I really think that the less you know about what goes on when you pick up the club and sling it in the general direction of the ball, the better off you're going to be. (On the other hand, the more your *opponent* knows, the worse off he'll be, but we'll get to that in a later chapter.)

Having said that, I will concede that there are a few flaws in club or body placement that even the best golfer will have difficulty compensating for later on during his swing. Fortunately, almost all of them are readily identifiable at the top of the backswing and are easy to correct (Figure 2-9), though I must quickly add that if you've had success with any of these positions, leave well enough alone!

I'm also not much of a believer in corrective drills and exercises, but if you insist on practicing basic swing movements, I'd much rather have you do some drills you'd actually enjoy (Figure 2-10) rather than struggling with dopey instructional doodads like that stupid club with a hinge in its shaft, or straining yourself trying to hit balls with a towel tucked under your armpit or your elbows wrapped together with a strap.

A PENNY FOR YOUR SWING THOUGHTS

No offense, but if you're like most golfers and I gave you a penny for your swing thoughts, I'd be wildly overpaying. "Toll the bell," "Swing in a barrel," "Hit against a firm left side" — honestly, where do people get this stuff?

The only images I've ever found at all useful as I swing the club back are to imagine that there is a spider the size of a Swedish meatball sitting out there in front of me instead of a golf ball, or that I am about to hit a large, gooey layer cake with a 2 X 4.

Swing Too Inside-out

Figure 2-9. Swing Faults to Look Out For. Ask a friend (*not* an opponent) to check you out and see if you're committing any of these swing sins.

Letting Go at the Top

Swing Too Flat

Figure 2-10. Practice Makes Perfect. Golf shouldn't be hard work. It's easy to "have a party" as you "groove" the key head (A), shoulder (B), and wrist (C) movements that provide 95 percent of the oomph in the bad golfer's swing.

A. The Head Turn. Keep your body fixed in position, and delay your head snap for as long as possible.

B. The Shoulder Heave. Move your whole upper body as you really *reach* for those hors d'oeuvres.

C. The Wrist Flip. Make sure you're pumping the martini shaker with your wrists, not swinging it with your arms.

CHAPTER 3

Making the Bad Golf Shots

THE SLICE

One of bad golf's few absolute fundamentals is that regardless of what club you use, when you hit a golf ball with a full swing it will do one of two things: either it will slice, or it will go straight but nowhere (Figure 3-1).

This condition holds true whether the ball is hit from a tee on the drive, or from a normal lie on the fairway, in the rough, or in a bunker, or if circumstances permit, from a tee in the fairway or rough or a bunker. (Short "touch" shots made with the hands gripping down on the club and the feet close together, or with the hands or feet themselves, are a different matter that I'll get into in a later chapter.)

Being able to depend on the natural propensity of a reasonably hard-hit golf ball to travel in a left-to-right direction is a great benefit for the bad golfer, and he accepts the 10 to 200 yards of lost distance a slice costs as a small price to pay for his peace of mind as he gets ready, say, to hit a 5-wood on a tricky little 114-yard par-3 water hole (Figure 3-2).

With this advantage in mind, most smart bad golfers figure out pretty early on that making a deliberate effort to cure a slice is like attempting to do something about a winning streak in Las Vegas. Fortunately, even if someone is loony enough to try, the golf lesson or instructional book he relies on for guidance can generally be counted on to derail his game so completely that he won't be able to hit the ball far enough to get into trouble.

In fact, the shot that bad golfers fear most is not the ball that goes off like a rocket at a 90-degree angle, but rather the score-wrecking, right-down-the-middle, 230-yard straight shot that can suddenly turn up without warning at the worst possible time.

The problem with the straight shot is that it can only be hit by accident. What usually happens is that you unconsciously slip into some bad "good" habits and suddenly start cracking out scary beauties long and strong right down the pipe, and the next thing you know, you have to punch a wedge out of someone's living room in a condo 150 feet beyond the left side of the hole. (I'll show how to hit that shot, too, later on in the book.)

You never know when a hard-to-shake spell of straight hitting is going to turn up, but there are some danger signs you can watch out for (Figure 3-3). Be particularly alert when you're relaxed and not paying any special attention to your swing—that's when those wild shots are most likely to creep in.

AIRBALL

HOOK ◄

FADE
PUSH
WIPE
LEAKER
CUT SHOT
TOED BALL
BANANA
CLASSIC SLICE
SHANK

Figure 3-1. Basic Ball Flight Patterns. The hook is included for reference purposes only.

Figure 3-2. Which Club? As the crow flies, it's 125 yards to the marker on this driving range, but don't pull out a 7-iron! Remember, with its looping trajectory, the sliced golf ball takes a "great circle route" to its target and thus has to travel *190* yards. Too bad we don't get frequent slicer miles!

Figure 3-3. Slice Wreckers. Rich Taylor, the pro at Scottsdale's famous Camelback Inn Golf Club, kindly consented to demonstrate some of the most treacherous shot-straightening swing moves. Beware of these "banana killers"!

Badly Delayed Uncocking of Wrists

Excessively Straight Left Arm

Head "Trapped" Behind Ball

Right Elbow Too Close to Side

The reason why golf is such a demanding game is a matter of simple physics. The golf ball has to be forced up into the air from a stationary position well below the level of the player's own center of gravity, which, depending on his build, is located anywhere from two to five feet *above* the golf ball. You don't have to be Albert "Fuzzy" Einstein (a 22-handicapper in his day and a *very* creative guy with a scorecard) to realize that hitting *down* on the ball isn't going to do the trick (Figure 3-4).

It's hard enough to hit up on a ball perched on a two-inch tee, but when it's on the ground, even if it's in a perfect lie, there's barely a half-inch of space along the bottom of the ball where the club can get a good angle on it and lever it up off the grass (Figure 3-5). Clearly, some means must be found to apply the clubhead to this tiny vulnerable spot on the ball's underside, and that's where the divot comes in.

The dipping, swaying, and heaving motions of the swing work together to produce the sharply downward clubhead trajectory that allows even a less lofted wood or a long iron to plow deeply into the turf behind the ball and work its way

Figure 3-4. A Matter of Gravity. If you drop your car keys, you don't retrieve them by smacking down on them with your palm (A); you pick them up with your hand (B). Golf is no different, except the car keys would probably take a sharp lateral kick into a storm drain.

into a position from which it can deliver the violent vertical strike that's needed to get it airborne (Figure 3-6).

The low point of the club's swing path is reached an inch or two before the ball itself is hit, when the club is moving upward after cutting an impressive swath through the intervening sod and propelling a clump of dislodged earth a considerable distance. (Occasionally, the divot actually travels farther than the ball itself, which is really only a problem on longer shots, like the drive.)

The size and shape of the divot that results from this ascending blow depends on the club used and the type of shot being made (Figure 3-7), but the principle remains the same—by removing a pound or two of grass and dirt from directly behind the ball, the ball itself has been, in effect, elevated, just as if it were placed on a tee. When conditions are favorable, the same result can, of course, be obtained by placing the ball on an actual tee.

Figure 3-5. The Hitting Quadrant. Less than 20 percent of the surface area of a golf ball is of any use at all in getting it airborne.

Figure 3-6. The Up-from-Under Below. By excavating a shallow trench directly behind the ball, the club is able to approach it on the proper ascending angle.

Figure 3-7. Typical Divots. The experienced golfer can tell a lot about a shot just by looking at the divot the player took when he made it, and let me tell you, all of these were beauties!

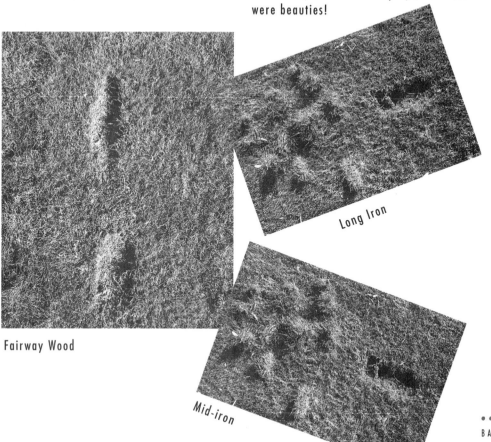

Long Iron

Fairway Wood

Mid-iron

THE SMASH

Although the ball-striking mechanics I've just outlined are relatively simple, they can be used to produce an amazing array of different shots, ranging from trick shots and finesse shots to trouble shots, deep trouble shots, and the all-too-often-forgotten "forgotten shot." I'll describe some of those in the next chapter when we get out onto the course, but for now I want to concentrate on the Smash, the Hack, and the Slash—the trio of indispensable golf shots that form the very foundation of the bad golfer's game.

First and foremost of these is the Smash, the all-or-nothing full-swing powerhouse clout used to belt the ball off the tee on long, wide-open holes, propelling it many dozens of yards in a mostly forward direction with awesome force (Figure 3-8).

The driver is nearly always used for the Smash, and ideally it should be one of those new oversized clubs with an extra long whippy graphite shaft and a head the size of an ingot. The aim here is to swing very, very hard. With the ball up on a tee, and acres of fairway beckoning, you owe it to yourself to "swing for the bleachers."

But a word of caution is in order. This swing needs plenty of room. I strongly recommend that other players remain seated on a bench off to the side of the tee, or in the cart, or in a prone position behind the cart, until the club comes to a complete stop, which sometimes does not occur until well after the swing is completed.

Figure 3-8. The Smash. In my setup for this shot (A), I've adopted a wider than usual stance, and I've taken the precaution of unlacing my shoes to give extra room for my power move. I've also removed my wristwatch to protect it from possible damage. At the top of my swing (B), you can clearly see how my unusually full body turn is pouring on the power as I prepare to really let out some shaft. Notice that after impact (C), even though I came completely out of my shoes, the toes are both pointing toward the target—a sure sign of a solid hit.

THE HACK

Unlike the Smash, where the hitting conditions are ideal and your confidence, even if misplaced, contributes to a good, free-swinging move into the ball, with the Hack your object is to use a highly controlled, abbreviated swing to overcome anxiety in one of the low-percentage playing situations that account for between 50 and 170 of the strokes in an average bad golfer's round.

Among these are less than perfect lies, long carries over hazards, and shots made into stiff headwinds. Whatever the challenge, the best response is to make as fast and as short a swing as you are capable of, thereby reducing to an absolute minimum the amount of time during which something serious can go wrong (Figure 3-9).

Another way to look at the shot is that you're trying to "beat your brain to the punch" by hitting the ball before you've had a chance to think of all the many thousands of things that could go wrong. In fact, in the four one-hundredths of a second it takes to hit the Hack, the average player can visualize no more than sixty separate negative outcomes.

Figure 3-9. The Hack. The correct stance for this shot (A) calls for your weight to be well back, with your head a foot or more behind the ball, and your body held rigid as if you were about to take a swat at an angry hornet that just landed on the ground in front of you.

In the backswing (B) the club is never brought more than waist high, and there should be a distinct feeling that the downswing has been nearly completed before the backswing has even begun.

Due to the tremendous acceleration of the club in the shortened downswing (C), the club often remains behind as the hands sweep up into a good high finish.

THE SLASH

This shot, which is designed to let you hit when your swing is blocked by an obstruction, like a clump of grass, a branch, patio furniture, or whatever, borders on being a specialty shot, but since the bad golfer, with his bold, unconventional play, so often finds himself stymied, I think it qualifies for inclusion among the bread-and-butter golf shots.

With its strange, jerky, unfinished motion, the Slash bears a superficial resemblance to the Hack, but it's a misleading one, because this is a radically different shot shaped to a specific purpose—the completion of some kind of swing when the ball is in a hopeless spot and circumstances do not favor its removal by more direct means.

Here, the best strategy is to eliminate the traditional backswing entirely and begin the hitting motion at the top (Figure 3-10). The club is held up at whatever angle the obstacle permits and waggled back and forth menacingly. The range of motion should be short and jumpy, and the club should be flung down suddenly and decisively, with as little premeditation as possible. The trick is to make the move when you least expect it. It isn't easy to fool yourself, but believe me, the element of surprise is essential to the success of the shot.

Figure 3-10. The Slash. In preparing to hit this shot (A), you want to have your weight well forward, with the whole body leaning into the shot, which insures a solid strike and leaves the right foot free to move laterally forward toward the ball if necessary.

After pausing for as much as a minute (B), the club is dropped onto the ball abruptly, and the body moves down and under.

A low-to-the-ground follow-through (C) permits the ball to be raked, tapped, or dragged, or even lobbed out with a motion that bears at least a passing resemblance to a golf swing.

Bad golfers are as capable of applying spin to the golf ball as the professionals are, but their ability to select or even predict in advance the particular type of spin they are going to impart to any given shot is not as well developed. In fact, in some special shots, like the shank, three or four different kinds of spin may be applied to the ball at the same time.

For this reason, I recommend that you forget about backspin, topspin, and sidespin, and concentrate instead on using *afterspin*, or body English as it is more popularly known, to influence the flight of the ball in the critical period following the moment of impact (Figure 3-11).

Remember that body English is most effective if applied immediately, and that it is far easier to modify the existing flight of the ball than to get it to change direction entirely or to begin moving again once it has come to a complete stop.

It's also imperative that you make up your mind as to exactly what you want the ball to do and communicate your wishes with unambiguous, coordinated body movements. Even though most high-handicappers recognize the vital importance of body English, they often make confused, contradictory, or unconvincing body movements to which no ball, no matter how compliant, can possibly respond.

All I can say is, if you're going to jump up and down and wave your arms around aimlessly in the equivalent of body Albanian or body Finnish, you'd really be better off just taking out a hanky and waving your ball good-bye.

Figure 3-11. Body English. There are four basic types of "afterspin": Comebackspin (A); Wrongsidespin (B); Forwardspin (C); and Stopspin (D).

A. Comebackspin prevents a ball that is bending too much to the right from turning any further. The player faces to the right, extends one or both arms at shoulder level with the hands sideways and the palms facing outward, and makes a series of rapid horizontal, right-to-left sweeping motions as if attempting to disperse a cloud of gnats.

B. Wrongsidespin causes a ball that is headed to the left to curve back to the right. The player bends into a half-crouch with most of his weight on a deeply flexed left knee, holds out his left arm with the palm facing forward, and performs one or more Quasimodo-like left-to-right clutching and wrenching motions. The right arm dangles uselessly at the side.

C. Forwardspin encourages a ball that is in danger of falling short to "hurry up" or "get legs." The player faces to the front and raises both arms directly above his head, palms facing out, and executes forward and downward pushing movements like the praying motions made by pagans worshipping an idol. For added effect, he may drop to his knees.

D. Stopspin halts the forward progress of a ball that's going too far and makes it "bite." The player's knees are bent, his arms are held out, palms down and parallel, with the fingers splayed apart and curved inward. The hands are moved from front to back in a distinct clawing motion, while the player jumps up and down with brisk, birdlike hops.

SHOULD YOU TALK TO YOUR BALL?

I'm not sure how effective verbal directions to your ball really are, because there are a lot of very stupid or very deaf golf balls out there, and if you don't believe me, take a look in any water hazard.

Still, as an adjunct to good body English, I don't see how it can do much harm. But it's important to keep in mind what kind of ball you're addressing. For example, if it's a $3.00 Slazenger with a balata cover that's headed for the woods, you might want to say forcefully (don't yell), "Oh, I say, do slow down, won't you please? There's a good ball."

On the other hand, an X-out can be exhorted more directly with a sharp command like "Bite, baby, bite!" And a range ball can be bid a fond adieu with a simple "Sayonara, sucker."

MULLIGANS

Every now and then you run into someone who refuses to honor the hallowed tradition of the Mulligan and insists that you play your first drive, even if it's a twenty-foot ground-pounding squirrel shot that burrows into the grass in front of the tee.

Whenever this happens, I just explain that I always make it my policy to hit the Mulligan *first*. That way, if the shot works out, no one is likely to protest, and if it doesn't work out, I simply go ahead and play my *real* shot, good-naturedly agreeing to forgo my right to take a Mulligan.

THE DO-OVER

Strictly speaking, the do-over is more of an honorable convention than a golf shot per se, but there's a good reason for treating it as one. Whether you want to hit a Mulligan from the tee, or have a redo of a skulled iron, or replay a chili-dipped wedge, or get a second chance at a six-foot putt you blew fifteen feet past the hole, you must convince someone—even if it's only yourself—that you are absolutely, positively entitled to a do-over.

To put it another way, even if you make an unbelievably bad shot, you can still rescue the situation by making a good, believable excuse. This calls for imagination, ingenuity, and cunning, but not surprisingly these are qualities that bad golfers invariably develop in their many years of profoundly inexpert play.

Now, when I say a believable excuse, I'm not talking about mealy-mouthed alibis like "my foot slipped" or "I knew I had the wrong club" or, worse still, misplaced admissions of guilt, such as "I didn't keep my left arm straight" or "I looked up."

What I'm referring to is a confident assertion that some clearly unfair condition or circumstance encountered out on the golf course was the sole basis for the uncharacteristic swing fault that produced a remarkably horrible shot. There are literally thousands of grounds for a legitimate complaint that is likely to be accepted by all but the most unreasonable player (Figure 3-12). Be creative. If you shank a wedge, call attention to the excessive hosel reticulation in the club; if you balloon a drive, mention the momentary spasm in the aurora borealis muscle of the anterior subdural follicle; and if you smother a wood, point out that miscalibrated crosscut mowing can result in club-grabbing "turflock."

Any one of these occurrences can provide a sufficient pretext for replaying a crummy shot, but just as the golf swing relies on a proper weight shift (whatever the hell that is), obtaining the undisputed right to a do-over depends on a well-executed blame shift (Figure 3-13). Don't nonchalant it. Believe me, you can save a lot more strokes with a good gripe than with a good grip.

Figure 3-12. Grounds for Complaint. Here are just a few samples of acceptable justifications for redoing a rotten shot. These compelling rationalizations fall into three broad categories: Equipment Failure (A), Temporary Infirmity (B), and Unwarranted Interference (C).

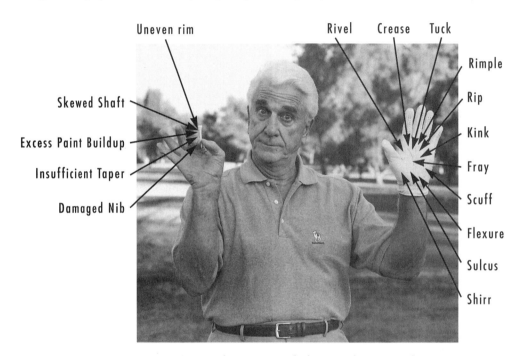

Uneven rim

Rivel Crease Tuck

Skewed Shaft

Rimple

Excess Paint Buildup

Rip

Insufficient Taper

Kink

Damaged Nib

Fray

Scuff

Flexure

Sulcus

Shirr

A. Equipment Failure. Due to slight irregularities in the manufacturing process, even a brand-new glove and a perfectly normal-looking tee can harbor hard-to-spot but serious flub-inducing flaws that no golfer should be penalized for.

B. Temporary Infirmity. You never know when a toothache is going to strike. It can suddenly kick in at the top of your swing and, boom, through no fault of your own your drive is in the woods. Then you tee up another ball, the pain mysteriously disappears, and you hit a beauty. Go figure.

C. Unwarranted Interference. You get used to a certain amount of distraction out on the course, and you accept it as part of the game, but an unexpected thoughtless outburst from some birdbrain can really throw off your tempo. Is that fair?

Figure 3-13. How to Make an Excuse. This is a four-part movement.

A. Expression of Dismay. Feelings of surprise and outrage are strongly voiced: surprise that a perfectly executed shot somehow went blooey, and outrage at the inequitable event that caused the mis-hit.

B. Citation of Cause. With as little delay as possible, a single, specific reason for the mis-hit is identified and condemned, in this case, a heretofore unnoticed hangnail that caused the grip to loosen at the top.

C. Appeal for Justice. An emotional request for the remedy of a replay is presented, along with any precedents, such as a previous do-over taken by a fellow player on an earlier hole.

D. Initiation of Replay. A forceful statement of an intent to replay the shot is made, coupled with an observation that, were the positions reversed, a do-over sought by a fellow player would be expeditiously granted.

CHAPTER 4

Taming the Course

THE WARM-UP

In this chapter, we'll take all of the bad golf fundamentals, put them together, and head out to the course. We're going to play a typical par-5 hole and see how a combination of course-management strategies and shot-making skills can bring even the most demanding track to its knees.

But before we get started, we're going to want to do a few simple exercises to make sure that when we get ready to hit, we're not so stiff that we end up suffering any actual injuries, which are no more effective in evoking sympathy than imaginary ones and are a lot less fun.

Most players use torso twists and club stretches for their warm-ups, and that's fine as far as it goes, but there are some specific muscles bad golfers rely on a great deal that need particular attention (Figure 4-1).

By the way, speaking of imaginary injuries, this is also an excellent time to introduce a spurious pull, strain, or sprain, or any other specious impairments that you plan on using during the round, and at the same time make a mental note of your fellow players' relative levels of agility and ease of movement for possible challenges of any dubious claims of disability they might try to introduce later on.

Figure 4-1. Getting the Kinks Out. Bad golf requires some unique hand (A), leg (B), upper-body (C), and lower-body (D) movements that can leave you pretty sore if you don't warm up properly.

A. They say golf is a left-handed game, but I find the right hand comes into play surprisingly often, and so I always make it a point to loosen up my throwing arm.

B. A powerful leg drive is the key to a good golf shot, and nowhere is this more true than when your ball is stuck behind a tree. Be sure you limber up that right leg with a couple of practice kicks.

C. Since you often have to really reach to draw a ball back in bounds with a club, or retrieve it from a hazard, or rake it out of a bunker, make sure you give those ligaments a good stretching.

D. Picking up a six-foot gimme while standing near the hole requires a coordinated motion of the arms, hips, and legs. A series of knee bends and back extensions will give you a nice, fast, supple, now-you-see-it-now-you-don't move.

FIRST SHOT: THE DRIVE

We're on the tee, ready to rip one right down the middle. It's early in the round, so I'm not going to uncork my Smash just yet. In fact, because I'm still not completely loose, I'm going to show some real self-control and take out the 3-wood.

This is a long hole, there's plenty of fairway out there, and I have a lot of leeway. My objective is simple—to get the heck off the tee and put the ball into play. Naturally, I'm going to swing easy and allow for my slice (Figure 4-2), but beyond that, can you guess what shot I'm going to hit?

I'll let you in on a little secret. Neither can I.

Figure 4-2. The Setup for the Drive. My powerful address position, with 75 percent of my weight on my right foot, 85 percent on my left foot, and the remaining 30 percent held in reserve, ready to swing into action at any moment, makes it look like I've teed up in front of the markers, but this is an optical illusion.

FIRST SHOT, PART II: THE MULLIGAN

As you can see (Figure 4-3), I drop-kicked my drive into the ladies' tee. I could easily play it from there, but since this is the first hole, I'm going to go ahead and take a Mulligan so you can get a full picture of how the game is played (Figure 4-4).

Incidentally, the thing to remember about Mulligans is that unlike other do-overs, you're entitled to hit them, so you don't need to come up with an excuse for why you should be allowed to take one, although I will say that in this case the photographer had a very noisy motor drive on her camera that really messed up my normally exquisite tempo.

Figure 4-3. The Knockdown Drive. By bouncing the clubhead firmly on the ground just before it made contact with the ball, I shaved some distance off my drive, but I also straightened out the shot. As it turns out, this unexpectedly conservative play makes a lot of sense, since the hole really opens up from the ladies' tee, and I can take all the trouble out of play on my second shot.

Figure 4-4. The Mulligan. I decided to play it safe and elected to hit an airball. It's a smart choice. My moonshot is sitting out there in the middle of the fairway just a shade or two short of 200 yards.

Figure 4-5. Ball in a Divot. If it's up to me, I just toss the ball out of here. I mean, it may be deep enough to qualify as a mini-bunker, but I don't see a tiny rake anywhere nearby, and it can't be a hazard since there's no row of little red or yellow toothpicks around it.

I've caught a bad break here. Although my ball is in the dead center of the fairway, it's also in the middle of a hole left by some jerk who didn't replace his divot (Figure 4-5).

No one in his right mind would make you play out of a lie like that, but if you've spent as much time on golf courses as I have, you've discovered by now that there are a lot of people out here who are not in their right minds, so I'm going to go ahead and show you how to make this shot.

The key is to insure that you get good contact with the ball, and to accomplish this, you must assume the correct stance (Figure 4-6). Before you start to work yourself into position, take out a 3-iron and start waggling it back and forth. This gives your hands something to do—and fellow players something to look at—while your feet go to work. But don't worry, we're not going to try to actually hit anything with the stupid thing.

Figure 4-6. The Divot Stance. As you make relaxed practice swings with a long iron, set your feet in a very narrow stance, "trapping" the ball between the toes of your shoes (A). Then, keeping your feet and legs together, lift the ball out of the divot and onto the grass (B).

A. The Trap. Your knees should touch, and your weight should be on your heels.

B. The Lift. Try to make one smooth "bunny-hopping" motion, rather than a series of kanga-roo bounces.

SECOND SHOT, THE SEQUEL: BALL SITTING UP NICELY IN FAIRWAY

Sometimes on closer inspection, a lie doesn't turn out to be quite as toxic as it first looked (Figure 4-7). I'm going to put the 3-iron back in the bag and take out a fairway wood instead. The percentage play is to hit the more lofted 5-wood rather than the 3-wood, since what you give up in yardage you more than make up for in consistency, but to keep things interesting, I'll go with the 3-wood and see if I can't advance the ball a bit (Figure 4-8).

Figure 4-7. Ball on Grass Right Behind Divot. Don't let the proximity of the ball to the divot hole rattle you. Hey, things could be worse—you could be in that damn thing.

Figure 4-8. The Midget-Killer. Even from a good lie, trying to get the ball up off the fairway with the flat 14-degree face of a 3-wood can lead you to hit behind the ball, so I've shrewdly chosen to top the shot instead. My wormburner ran a good 180 yards, but it ended up in a fairway bunker because of a bad bounce. Well, I guess when a shot has 50 to 75 bounces, you've got to figure there's going to be a rotten one in there somewhere.

THIRD SHOT: BALL IN FAIRWAY BUNKER

The most important thing to remember about shots hit from sand traps is that they aren't over until the ball actually leaves the bunker or you stop swinging. Because of this important fact, before you step in there and get ready to hit, you're going to want to make a few "around-the-world"-style 360-degree loop-de-loops with the club (Figure 4-9). This motion is a little like the practice swing I demonstrated in Chapter 2, but it is a continuous, uninterrupted movement, and, as we'll see in a moment, it has a slightly different purpose.

Now, when your ball ends up in a fairway bunker with a long way to go to the green, as mine has, you have two basic objectives: to make absolutely sure that the ball gets out of the bunker, no matter what, and to hit it as far as you possibly can.

These imperatives may seem contradictory, but you have plenty of time to resolve the apparent conflict at the top of your backswing when you finally decide whether you're going to clip the ball out clean, explode it out, or dig the head of the club deeply into the sand a foot behind the ball.

Since it's really too early to commit to one of these shots at the time the club is chosen, I'm going to use a 6-iron, which can hit the ball anywhere from a full 150 to a more controlled 0 yards, depending on the swing I select (Figure 4-10).

Figure 4-9. The Windmill Practice Swing. This is a somewhat unorthodox movement in that the club goes completely around the head and the feet steadily advance in whatever direction the ball travels.

Figure 4-9. The Windmill Practice Swing (continued).

Figure 4-10. The Dunch. Decision time. What's it going to be—go for the soft plop into the center of the fairway or the all-out shot most of the way to the green? The hell with it. I'm going to hit this sucker stiff to the pin.

THIRD SHOT, CONTINUED: BALL STILL IN BUNKER

As I advance through the bunker "herding" the ball toward its inevitable exit from the sand with my patented "cow-punch" lariatlike rotary shot, it may seem that I am making multiple swats at a moving ball rolling back at me as it fails repeatedly to clear the lip of the bunker, but the miracle of high-speed stop-action photography (Figure 4-11) clearly shows that I'm performing a single, unbroken rotary motion.

It may take a while to get out of the bunker successfully, but by not being in a hurry and by maintaining a constant, measured, almost monotonous swinging action, there's no doubt in my mind that I ended up saving several strokes.

Figure 4-11. The Windmill in Action. To an onlooker, this is all a blur of smooth, seamless motion, and only the fastest camera can capture the subtle shift from the theoretical "end" of one swing to the "beginning" of the next. As a practical matter, of course, this is a true "one-piece" swing.

FOURTH SHOT: BALL ABOVE FEET

In the playing areas of even the flattest courses, there are a surprising number of mounds, valleys, ridges, knolls, ravines, and hollows that you'd think they would have leveled out and filled in when they were bulldozing the fairways. Golfers have to learn how to contend with these powerful reminders of just how sloppy much golf course construction is.

Areas right around bunkers are notoriously uneven, and my ball has ended up just outside the edge of the trap in a severe upslope. It's not a pretty sight, but there's no reason to let a lie like this get the better of you. The trick here is to compensate for the awkward ball position by making adjustments in your stance and the placement of your hands on the club (Figure 4-12).

Once you get comfortable over the ball, you can take a surprisingly good cut at it with a roundhouse baseball-style swing. In a way, it's just like hitting an unbelievably slow pitch hanging there right in the center of the strike zone (Figure 4-13). Batter up! Plaaaaaaay golf!

Figure 4-12. Setting up for the Sidehill Shot. By bending my knees sharply and choking way down on the club, I've compensated for the awkward lie and gotten close enough to the ball to really feel confident about the shot.

Figure 4-13. Fairway Wood from Sidehill Lie. On second thought, I think I can hit this with a 5-wood. You can never be sure where the slope is going to send the ball when you hit from an odd angle like this, but there's only one way to find out. Belt it!

I hit a solid line drive, but I pulled it toward the third base line, and now my ball is stymied behind a tree (Figure 4-14). I clearly have no choice but to make a recovery shot.

When you're confronted with a lie like this, you need to make up your mind right away whether you're going to go for accuracy (Figure 4-15) or distance (Figure 4-16), as I've decided to do here. Either way, this situation calls for a shot that uses a lot of right hand and depends entirely on "touch" and "feel." The club plays a very passive role. In fact, you really want to have the sense that you aren't swinging it at all.

When you decide to go for distance, as I did here, keep in mind that even with a major-league move, the ball is only going to go about as far as a decently hit 9-iron, but this is still the percentage play, because it is definitely going to go a couple of hundred feet further than a sclaffed 9-iron, and honestly, when was the last time you accidentally threw a ball straight into the ground ten inches in front of your left foot?

Figure 4-14. The Stymie. The only way I'm going to get the ball out of here is to pick it up cleanly and "let it fly."

Figure 4-15. The Lob. If you're just trying to make sure you end up safely in the fairway, make a shallow underarm swing with the wrist stiff and the elbow bent, and use only the forearm and a little upward hip shift to provide the power. You may want to cradle the club in the left hand to add some extra balance to the movement.

Figure 4-16. The Full Pitch. If you see daylight and decide to go for it, you should make a full shoulder turn, extend your right arm, and let the wrist snap at release. Notice that the club is completely grounded during the entire shot.

FURFTH SHOT: BALL IN DEEP ROUGH

I may have been a bit greedy when I pegged the ball toward the flag instead of out into the fairway. It didn't even make the first cut, and now it's in super-heavy grass.

Well, there's no need to waste time beating around the bush. Let's pop that thing out into the short grass (Figure 4-17).

Figure 4-17. The Wedgie. There's nothing to this shot. Use your left leg as a brace, bend your right knee, and concentrate on hitting the ball crisply off the toe. Don't try to "lace it" or you could end up booting it deeper into the rough or hitting a "clodhopper" that doesn't get all the way out, and then you're stuck having to "tootsie" the ball into the fairway with a series of telltale shoe-taps.

FRUTH SHOT: LONG CARRY OVER WATER

The sight of a gleaming sheet of water between the ball and the hole is only daunting to the golfer who is afraid that his ball won't make it across. This apprehension leads to a very common misplay: wasting a shot by hitting a lay-up short of the water rather than going for it. Yes, you'll be making your next shot from a spot a lot nearer the hazard, and you'll have less water to cross, but standing that close to it you'll also have a much better view of the wet stuff, and that just increases your anxiety.

The bad golfer, by contrast, suffers from no such concerns. He *knows* that his ball is going to hit the water, and consequently he plays a shot that stands an excellent chance of reaching the other side, even if it does get a little damp in the process (Figure 4-18).

Figure 4-18. The Waterbeater. A very fast short swing using five or six more clubs than the distance calls for will rocket the ball off the ground low and hot, sending it skipping across the surface of the water like a souped-up hydroplane.

FUFFT SHOT: BALL IN WATER

My shot came up just a bit short (Figure 4-19), but thanks to the fifteenth club in my bag—the trusty ball retriever—I'm actually sitting pretty, if a little bit soggy. With its longer-than-usual shaft and concave face, this very useful "stick" necessitates a few minor changes in the grip and requires a slow, fuller swing, but it's an easy move to get the hang of (Figure 4-20).

Figure 4-19. The Liquid Lie. There's no need to take a penalty in a situation like this—that ball is eminently playable.

Figure 4-20. The Fling Shot. Grip the retriever with your hands about a foot apart and play the ball way back in your stance. Once you've securely snared it in the cup, sweep the ball up and out of the water, then sling it forward with a smooth casting action, releasing it at the end of the swing.

FIRFF SHOT: THE FOOLPROOF 5-IRON

The ball's in the fairway, and I'm in the clear, about 155 yards from the green—it's a textbook shot with the bad golfer's best friend, the super-reliable 5-iron (Figure 4-21). As long as I don't shank this puppy, I'm home free, putting for par.

Figure 4-21. The Shank. If the awesome power of this explosive lateral shot could be harnessed, we could all play an extremely effective—if somewhat odd-looking—game of golf.

FOOTH SHOT: BALL IN CONDOMINIUM

. . . .

If you've practiced any carpet-putting in the winter months when the weather is lousy and you can't get out onto the course, this "Texas Wedge" shot hit off a patch of rug with a putter is an absolute breeze (Figure 4-22).

I don't want to get sidetracked into a lengthy discussion of the rules, but let me mention in passing that if the ball had ended up wedged in a sofa cushion, or sitting in a candy dish, or blocked by a lamp, that would all be classified as Casual Decor, and you take a drop on the rug. Also, to avoid causing any instances of House under Repair, you can always open a door or window before making your shot.

Figure 4-22. The Carpet Runner. Play the ball in the center of your stance and make the same swing with the putter you'd use for a stubbed chip. You want to hit down on the ball and pinch it slightly, but bear in mind that shag carpeting has a tendency to grab the clubhead and twist it open, and the ball will often fly in a strongly right-to-left direction when hit out of a hooked rug.

FREE DROP: BALL ON CART PATH

My ball is sitting in the cart path, so I'm entitled to a free drop. While we're on the subject of rules, the regulation says you're supposed to hold the ball at shoulder height and arm's length and drop it, but the question of velocity isn't covered at all.

The way I see it, meteors drop into the earth's atmosphere at upward of 20,000 mph, and even an ordinary piano dropped from the upper story of an apartment building is going to be traveling at a pretty good clip when it hits the ground. It's clear you have a lot of leeway (Figure 4-23).

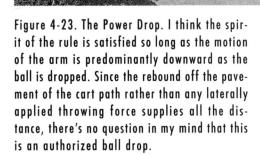

Figure 4-23. The Power Drop. I think the spirit of the rule is satisfied so long as the motion of the arm is predominantly downward as the ball is dropped. Since the rebound off the pavement of the cart path rather than any laterally applied throwing force supplies all the distance, there's no question in my mind that this is an authorized ball drop.

FUMPH SHOT: THE APPROACH FROM 100 YARDS IN

When you're 75 to 100 yards from the green and there's no real trouble between you and the pin, how do you decide whether to make a high, soft pitch or a flatter, bump-and-run-style pitch?

The answer is surprisingly simple: *you don't decide.* Take out a pitching wedge, address the ball, and keep your mind clear. The secret of this shot is that it's a secret—it must come to you as a complete surprise (Figure 4-24). It's the sudden moment of panic about halfway through your downswing that supplies the power and the pin-seeking, radarlike accuracy that make this shot so intimidating.

Figure 4-24. The Chippitch or Pitchip. As I take the club back, I haven't got a clue what I'm going to do with this shot. At the top of my backswing, I'm still weighing the alternatives. When the club is about three feet from the ball (left), I make up my mind—I'm going to chitch it (below)! Well, maybe I should have chutted it or puttched it.

The bunker shot scares the daylights out of most players but it really doesn't faze the bad golfer because he understands a very important thing about the way the classic sand trap explosion shot works—it doesn't.

With this in mind, I recommend a more straightforward approach to getting the ball off the "beach" and onto the "dance floor" (Figure 4-25). I should add

that this play is really designed for deep, steep-sided hell bunkers where the only things that are visible to a fellow player as you make the shot are your head, a little of your shoulders, and the club as it swings back to the top of your backswing and then up at the end of your follow-through. In shallower sand traps, I'd stick with the old reliable Windmill.

Figure 4-25. The Hand Wedge. Once you realize that the mechanics of getting a ball out of sand depend on the club never actually touching the ball, this shot is a breeze. As you swing down to the ball (above), take your right hand off the club and reach down and scoop up the ball and a handful of sand. Swing the club up with your left hand, and toss the ball and the sand up and onto the green with a right-handed underarm toss (right).

SIXTH SHOT: THE TWENTY-FOOT GIMME

At first blush, this putt (Figure 4-26) probably looks a shade too long to pick up, but appearances can be deceiving.

Let's look at things from a different angle, down at ground level where the action is and where we can get a more accurate picture of the situation (Figure 4-27).

I must say I hit some pretty memorable shots on this hole, and it would have been something to round it all out by draining a twenty-foot tap-in putt, but to tell you the truth, I'm just as happy to pick it up and ice my very respectable bogey 6 with no further ado!

Figure 4-26. A Real Knee-Knocker. A putt like this can be very intimidating unless you know how to "read the green" to determine whether you're entitled to a "break."

Figure 4-27. A Gimme's-Eye-View. If you align yourself along the actual path the ball would travel on its way to the cup (above), you can immediately see that this putt is laughably close to the hole (left). I'd have to be nuts to putt it! Let's pick this baby up!

CHAPTER 5

Mastering the Mind Game

THE OPPONENT

Golf would be difficult enough if all you had to do was go to the driving range and hit about a hundred balls some reasonable distance in a more or less straight direction. The need to make dozens and dozens of different kinds of shots out on a course that was deliberately designed to punish all but the most flawless hit greatly complicates matters. Add in all the basic forces of the universe that conspire to misdirect and sap distance from your shots—gravity, electromagnetism, entropy, intertia, the strong atomic force, the weak force, and whatever causes underwear to ride up—and you really have to bear down to put together a halfway decent round.

Yet all of these obstacles pale by comparison to the ultimate challenge in the game of golf: playing a match against an actual living, breathing opponent (Figure 5-1). Now your two most implacable foes—the ball and the course—are joined by a third and truly formidable antagonist: a fellow golfer.

Figure 5-1. The Opponent. Beneath a "friendly" competitor's relaxed and affable exterior (left) lurks a wild and ruthless monster (right) who will stop at nothing in his desperate effort to score a little better than you, even if he just barely edges out your heroic, never-say-die 137 with a slop-luck, can't-miss-a-putt, once-in-a-lifetime 136.

It is a bitter irony that the very person who would seem most likely to be your natural ally—a fellow sufferer at the hands of this heartless game—is transformed by circumstance into a committed adversary who stubbornly opposes the creative rules interpretations and generous attitude toward gimmes and Mulligans that he should vigorously applaud.

And what causes this poisonous metamorphosis that turns an easygoing individual just out to have a little fun on the links into a grim-faced rival dedicated to your downfall? The answer lies at the very core of golf, and it is without doubt the game's oldest and saddest truth: The only way a golfer can derive any satisfaction whatsoever from scoring a 9 on a short par-4 is if whoever he is playing with gets a 10.

THE MENTAL GAME

Unlike some other competitive sports that require brute force and superb physical conditioning, golf relies primarily on raw brainpower, although brute force may be needed from time to time if, for example, you have to drive a ball directly through the trunk of a tree or an inconveniently placed lawn ornament. Some physical conditioning can also come in handy if you arrive on the course at 7:54 for a 7:55 tee time.

The fact that golf is principally a mental game is readily conceded by every player (even ones who won't concede much of anything else, particularly tiny little ten-footers), but golfers would much rather spend endless minutes working on their short games instead of investing a little time and effort into improving the psychological side of their play.

That's really a pity, because the key to playing winning golf does not lie in taking strokes off *your* score, but rather in getting your opponent to add strokes to *his* score.

Do you have the intellectual capacity, the mental toughness, the sheer course smarts to come out on top in a hard-fought, take-no-prisoners golf match with a plainly superior player? Take the short quiz below (Figure 5-2). If you get a less than perfect score, you might want to consider pursuing a less demanding recreational activity, like fee-fishing or slot-car racing.

Figure 5-2. A Quick Quiz. Take a look at the five pictures below, and then answer the questions. Turn the page upside down for the correct answers.

I. You and your opponent both hit your balls into this bunker. They're the identical brand and have the same number and no distinguishing marks. Which one is yours?

Ball (A) [ ]   Ball (B) [ ]

II. You're standing next to a sprinkler head, and an opponent asks you for the yardage. Do you read it right side up and tell him it's 186 yards, or accidentally read it upside down and tell him it's 981 yards?

(A) 186 yards [ ]   (B) 981 Yards [ ]

III. Your opponent has hit his ball into the wooded area pictured below. Do you think you could find it for him?

(A) YES [ ]   (B) NO [ ]

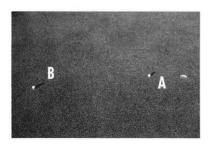

IV. There are two balls on the green: your opponent's (A) and yours (B). In your considered opinion, which one is unquestionably a gimme?

(A) Your opponent's ball [ ]   (B) Your ball [ ]

I. B; II. B; III. B; IV. B

UNCONSCIOUS GOLF

Every bad golfer has had the experience of hitting a few shots, or playing a hole or two, or even part of a whole round, where everything just seemed to click. It makes you wonder if there isn't some positive mental technique, like self-hypnosis or some form of Zen training, that you could use on yourself so you could play "unconscious" golf all the time.

Alas, I have my doubts. For one thing, if you're conscious of the fact that you are unconscious, then you're already much too aware of things for it to do much good, and if you're unconscious of the fact you're unconscious, you'll be in a coma and you're going to hit the ground long before you hit the ball. I suppose you could hypnotize yourself (and I'll leave aside for now the problem of how exactly you're going to unhypnotize yourself on the way to the bar at the end of the round), but if you go around in a trance, a lot of guys are going to play tricks on you like tying your shoelaces together while you're not looking, or slipping you one of those exploding golf balls.

And as for Zen, if you're planning to meditate before every shot, I'd say we're looking at an eleven-hour round, and even the marshalls at Pebble Beach might have a problem with that. And if you do get "enlightened," you're just going to see the utter futility of the whole game of golf and give it up and go off somewhere and bang gongs and raise a bunch of those little pine trees the size of shaving brushes.

INNER OUTER GOLF

Although the art and practice of golf psychology (or psychogolfology, as I prefer to call it) is an incredibly complex subject, all of its techniques are predicated on the same underlying premise: Since you can't beat your opponent, you must concentrate your efforts on getting your opponent to defeat himself.

Is this unsportsmanlike? Give me a break. There you are, confronted by a grossly unequal contest in which, even allowing for your gigantic handicap, you're badly outgunned by a far superior player. This guy is going to throw all kinds of low-down, dirty stuff at you—220-yard drives, magnificent iron shots, amazing triple-break putts. He'll have no shame and show no mercy.

Knowing all this, you can't tell me you're not entitled to do everything within your power to level—or, if necessary, plant mines on—the playing field, thereby transforming a hopelessly lopsided match with a good, semi-good, or not entire-

Figure 5-3. The Limp (A) and the Twitch (B). The aim of these two relatively innocuous devices is to give your opponent the unsettling feeling that he is picking on a cripple who may also be a nutcase.

A. The Limp can be anything from a major move in which the knee collapses completely to just an understated shift of the weight to the toe of one foot. In both cases, the effect is diminished if you change the leg or foot you limp on halfway through the round.

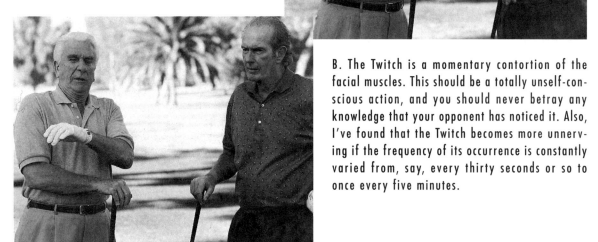

B. The Twitch is a momentary contortion of the facial muscles. This should be a totally unself-conscious action, and you should never betray any knowledge that your opponent has noticed it. Also, I've found that the Twitch becomes more unnerving if the frequency of its occurrence is constantly varied from, say, every thirty seconds or so to once every five minutes.

Figure 5-4. The Wince (A), the Lookaway (B), and the Crouch (C). These seemingly unrelated moves all have exactly the same purpose: to give your opponent the idea that there is something terribly wrong with his swing even if he's happy with the results.

A. The Wince. The expression you're looking for here is a mixture of shock and sympathy, something along the lines of what you might produce involuntarily after seeing a kitten run over by a dump truck.

B. The Lookaway. Here you want to make a sudden dramatic turning movement of your head and upper body, just as if you were Dracula averting his eyes from a crucifix or shielding his face from a sudden shaft of vampire-killing sunlight.

C. The Crouch. Even if your opponent is a straight hitter, sooner or later he's bound to let one get away from him. After he sprays that wild shot off at an angle, make a point for the next hole or two of ostentatiously "taking cover."

ly rotten golfer into a genuinely one-sided competition much more in your favor—the two of you against him.

The methods employed by resourceful bad golfers to make the most of their limited playing skills in tense matchplay situations fall into three basic categories: passive strategies (Inner Outer Golf), active tactics (Outer Inner Golf), and total psychological warfare (Outer Outer Golf).

The first of these systems, Inner Outer Golf, uses repetitions of subtle personal quirks, habits, and peculiarities that are carefully concocted to lower your opponent's self-esteem (Figure 5-3), undermine his confidence (Figure 5-4), and ruin his timing (Figure 5-5).

Note that while all of these mannerisms were obviously fabricated for the occasion, they are completely innocent and probably wouldn't bother your opponent in the least if he were minding his own business instead of keeping his eye on you all the time trying to catch you in some stupid minor rules infraction.

Figure 5-5. The Fidget (A), the Time Check (B), and the Hurry-up (C). The goal of these aggravating gestures is to convey to your opponent the unmistakable impression that he is playing ridiculously slow golf. I used to use the Yawn here, too, but it can be surprisingly contagious, and you and everyone else can end up with an actual uncontrollable yawn.

A. The Fidget. This can be any nervous or impatient fiddling activity, like cracking your knuckles, obsessively cleaning your nails with a tee, or idly flipping a coin. Here I'm performing the Queeg, the classic three-ball palm-and-finger-roll pioneered by Humphrey Bogart, an excellent golfer who perfected this classic routine out on the course years before he used it in *The Caine Mutiny*.

B. The Furtive and Not-So-Furtive Time Check. As with the Twitch, you want to be a little unpredictable in how often you make these watch-reading moves, and you should never make eye contact with your opponent or any direct, pointed, or rude motion calling his attention to your agitated state. The Furtive Check (above) is just a brief head-twist, coupled with a clockwise turn of the left wrist. In the Not-So-Furtive Check (right), bend the elbow and sweep the whole arm forward until it's in front of your face.

C. The Hurry-up. The better your timing is with this movement, the more dramatic will be its impact on your opponent's tempo. Always poise yourself so that you can begin walking the instant he hits the ball (left). As soon as you hear the sound of impact, immediately step off on your lead foot and begin striding purposefully away (below).

ALL BETS ARE OFF

I'm not much of a fan of betting on golf, even in the insignificant amounts that most people play for. It slows things down, and makes picky golfers even pickier about little details like the totally irrelevant fact that the ball you found in the rough right where yours should have been isn't the same color as the one you hit from the tee.

Still, you don't want to be a spoilsport (unless, of course, you think it will annoy a rival enough to throw him off his game), so I go along with a $2 Nassau or Skins or whatever, but I propose a few one-cent "trash" bets of my own just to keep the fun in the game. The stakes are so paltry, nobody wonders what a "Pantsie" or a "Nosie" or any of the rest of them are.

This is a great way to get rid of all the pennies in your pocket, because the idea here is to constantly interrupt your opponent's play by paying him for incomprehensible victories you invent on the spot, like "Even-Steven" (hitting an even-numbered shot with an even-numbered club), "Rakie-Dakies" (having a ball come to rest against a sand trap rake), and "Markie-Mark" (hitting a ball next to a sprinkler head or yardage stake).

Even though you're forking over the moolah — well, the minimoolah — this can become surprisingly irritating to an opponent. If he asks you to stop, you can quickly agree that "all bets are off," and probably save yourself a few bucks from that Nassau you stood a good chance of losing, and all for the cost of a handful of pennies.

Oh, yes. "Pantsie" is for ugliest trousers, and "Nosie" is for a visible piece of snot in one nostril (it's "Double-Nosies" for two).

OUTER INNER GOLF

If a score-crazy opponent starts applying the pressure with a vicious string of pars or a ruthless birdie or two, you're going to have to rachet up the intensity of your own defensive play to a new level and begin a campaign of deliberate distraction.

That means using active tactics to directly destroy his concentration (Figure 5-6) and sabotage his shot-making skills (Figure 5-7).

Since these expedients could be construed as being a bit below the belt, you should recognize that you're opening yourself up to retaliation, but frankly, this is only fair. You have moved the match to a more aggressive mode, and your opponent is clearly entitled to make his own attempts to distract you.

This need not be a source of major concern. His efforts will most likely pale by comparison with your polished disruptive play, and even if he does give as good as he gets, your erratic, unstable jabbing movement is inherently much harder to derail than his single-minded, machinelike repeatable swing. (In fact, your basic motion may actually be *improved* by a well-timed, if ill-intended, interruption.)

Of course, if you have undergone extensive insensitivity training as I have, nothing short of actual gunplay will have any discernible negative effect on your game.

Figure 5-6. The Rattle (A) and the Tiptoe (B). The nice thing about noisemaking is that even if your opponent knows it's coming, it still works, and if he's a particularly high-strung individual, the anticipation can actually increase the effectiveness of the interruption.

A. The Rattle (left). Out on the course, you're pretty much confined to jiggling the clubs if you want to make a not-too-outrageous racket, but on the tee you have the ballwasher, which is a major acoustic asset. The timing of the sound-producing move and the impression that it was unintentional are both critical to the success of this procedure.

B. The Tiptoe (right). Respond to your opponent's inevitable dirty look or angry remark by adopting an exaggerated, super-quiet, "don't wake the baby" method of walking. Maintain this "silent treatment" for as long as you feel it retains its capacity to irritate.

LUCK IS A FOUR-LETTER WORD

It's generally a lot more discouraging for you to lose a hole to an expert player who hits a perfect approach shot that lands softly on the green and then spins back into the hole than it is for a good golfer to be beaten by that freak shank of yours that caromed off a rock, banged into the flagstick at 40 mph, then dropped in the cup. After all, his was pure skill, and yours was dumb luck, right?

Maybe not. As long as you act as though the shot came as no surprise and pretend to be completely satisfied with your remarkable albeit bizarre play, you can plant in his mind the troubling notion that your game may have hitherto unplumbed depths.

That's why I never make any disparaging comments about shots I hit until after they stop rolling, no matter how atrocious they are (assuming, that is, that I'm not planning to file a claim for a do-over). Who knows? The thing might work out, and I can affirm with charming humility, that, yes, give or take a ricochet or two, I *did* plan to play a smothered "Neanderthal" skull shot off the equipment shed—hey, those hours of practice behind the garage really paid off!

And if I snap-fade a ball into the woods and it doesn't come rocketing back out, I just shake my head and say, "Damn, I caught a pine tree—you can't get decent rebound off conifer bark." Or if one of my patented cut-punch sawbladed 4-irons skips twice on the water, then sinks like a stone, I remark irritably, "Algae—it just takes all the topspin off the ball."

It really does, you know.

Figure 5-7. The Cough (A), the Stifle (B), and the Boomer (C). I take justifiable pride in my ability to produce at will a very extensive repertoire of explosive physical sounds, but a more modest command of the various organs in your body's "orchestra" can serve your purposes. Incidentally, although I've illustrated the Cough here, the Sneeze works on exactly the same principle, but it's a bit more work. I advise against the Hiccup; like the Yawn, you can give yourself a case of the real thing if you aren't careful.

A. The Cough. At some point during play when your opponent is in between shots, and thus not expecting any baroque displays of odd behavior, suddenly break into an extended fit of hacking and wheezing. The fact that this episode did not come during his backswing adds credibility to the attack.

B. The Stifle. As your opponent prepares to hit, puff out your cheeks, place a hand over your mouth, and twist your torso as if you're making a superhuman effort to control an irresistible urge to cough until he has completed his swing. Make whatever low groaning or whining noises you deem necessary to call your dilemma to his attention.

C. The Boomer. This is really optional, since the Stifle itself will unnerve almost any golfer, but if you can produce, through natural or artificial means, a convincing fart at the very top of his swing, by all means do so.

OUTER OUTER GOLF

· ·

If the comparatively restrained techniques of Inner Outer and Outer Inner Golf fail to achieve the desired result, it may become necessary to try a different tack.

Instead of attempting to wreak havoc on only a few limited areas of an opponent's mental makeup or producing individually tailored distractions at specific points in his play, you may decide it's time to launch an all-out assault on his fundamental sense of well-being and replace it with a nagging and immediate concern for his own personal safety.

Over the years, I've had success with quite a few methods of convincing an opponent that there is a real chance that he will not live to complete the round (Figure 5-8), but, as a purist, I've always sought some means of inducing terminal paranoia that required no props or special dress or other elaborate equipment of any kind.

That's why I now prefer to "bug" my opponents by sharing with them the latest information about the dread Death's Head Spider Mite, an almost microscopically small, practically invisible insect (it's no larger than the period at the end of this sentence) that infests golf courses throughout North America and spreads cellular mitosis or "Slime Disease," an ailment as incurable as it is nonexistent (Hmm, where did that period go, anyway?)

This hideous malady has deceptively mild early symptoms—white spots under the fingernails, an inability to remember people's names when you first meet them, sudden headaches after quickly consuming large amounts of ice cream, and a strange sense of depletion after sex—but soon progresses to the fatal final stages of cerebral jellosis, when the brain turns to mush. A total cranial skullectomy is the only treatment. (I like to mention that one sufferer who had such a transplant lived for a month with the head of a baboon—if you call it living.)

The beauty of this approach is that since this infinitesimal fictional bug closely resembles a freckle (unless it has already burrowed under the skin, in which case its protruding tail looks exactly like an arm hair) you never need to produce one (Figure 5-9).

Interestingly, the costly, painful, but 100 percent effective Slime Disease–preventing vaccination that I took the precaution of having leaves a scar that looks exactly like one I got when I fell off a horse when I was twelve. Who knows—yours might leave no scar at all.

Frankly, I think it's an extremely generous gesture on my part to make this staggeringly potent ploy available to the readers of this book. And to all of you cynics who say that the only reason I am letting you in on this technique is because I have discovered something even better, all I can say is, O ye of little faith, how right you are.

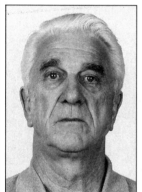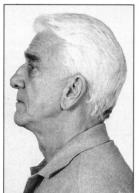

Figure 5-8. The Hit Parade. These are my all-time favorite scare tactics. I had a number of copies of the fake wanted poster (left) printed up, and would arrange for one to fall out of my golf bag when I took out a new glove. The fine print described an armed and dangerous psychotic killer who was suffering from the delusion that he was Leslie Nielsen. The Ozone Suit (right), meant to shield the wearer from the lethal ultraviolet rays of the sun during an Ozone Hole Alert, convinced anyone not equally well protected that they'd get skin cancer in about ten minutes flat, and they'd hit their balls deliberately under the shade of trees. It replaced the Radiation Suit, which I used with a dummy Geiger counter set to click more and more wildly at the turn of a hidden dial that I would twist as I got closer to an opponent's ball. They were all fun, but really much too clumsy.

Figure 5-9. The Bug. A helpful confederate to enlist in your campaign to get your opponent's mind off the match and onto the more important matter of his continued survival is the minuscule but deadly Death's Head Spider Mite. Begin by meticulously examining yourself for a possible infestation by this imaginary bug (top). During this preliminary stage of paranoia production, resist the urge to comment on what you're doing so your opponent's natural curiosity can build to a satisfactory level. A little later on (center), pretend to find one of the hellish insects, and react with exaggerated alarm. The final step (bottom) in the procedure involves "discovering" one of the creatures on your opponent and pointing out to him that although the bug's preferred habitat is underbrush, wooded areas, and high grass, millions of them can be found in one square foot of fairway.

A PICTURE IS WORTH A THOUSAND NEEDLES

Making innocent-sounding but deeply unhelpful observations about a rival's style of play, or passing on a tip or a swing thought that you know from experience to be completely lethal are time-honored methods of causing an adversary to implode.

Sadly, most of the classics, like complimenting an opponent on his steady head, or asking why he seems to pause at the top of his swing, or showing him your new "power pinkie" grip have been so overused that they really don't bother anyone any more.

That's why I've switched almost entirely to a more high-tech approach—asking an opponent his permission to film his flawless, syrupy-smooth swing for posterity and for my own personal home study. It goes without saying that no one ever refuses this flattering request.

A video camera is ideal for this gambit, but a cheap throwaway instamatic works almost as well. Obviously, you don't need any film, but bright lights and flashbulbs are a big plus.

I think I need hardly mention that to accurately record his memorable swing motion, the pictures cannot be staged during practice swings—they absolutely have to be totally candid and unrehearsed, and naturally the only way to achieve this result it to take the photos at an entirely unexpected, unguarded moment.

CHAPTER 6

Playing to Win

THE MATCH

Although it's certainly true that in the final analysis an opponent can only be defeated by one person—himself—I strongly believe you should assist him in this process in any way you can.

As we've seen, the mental side of golf gives you an excellent way to help your opponent get the better of himself, but it's a sad fact that a significant percentage of golfers are almost totally immune to the mind game, either because they don't actually have minds (Figure 6-1) or because they are naturally insensitive, or graduates of formal insensitivity training programs, or self-taught, as I am (Figure 6-2).

In cases like this, sooner or later you're going to have to adopt a much more hands-on type of strategy aimed at directly influencing the outcome of the match. And I'd say you're better off doing it sooner rather than later, because if you let

a hard-to-rattle opponent get away with his usual hey-diddle-diddle-right-down-the-middle, wake-me-when-it's-over style of play, you're going to suddenly discover you're five down with two holes to play, and you'll have to come up with some exceptional bad golf to eke out a victory.

Figure 6-1. Type "A" Golfer: "Clueless." You're wasting your time playing mind games with this guy, because the only thing you can do with what's in his head is inflate an average-sized automobile tire.

DRIVING FOR DOUGH

There's an old saying in golf, "Drive for show, putt for dough." I definitely agree that long straight drives aren't all that important (they certainly don't play a major role in my game), and there's no question in my mind that the green is where the action is. Still, I'd amend that aphorism to read, "Drive for dough, and pick up putts for dough."

Of course, I'm talking about driving the cart, not the ball, and as we'll see later in this chapter, I believe the key to the putter is using the back of it to scoop up the ball instead of fooling around with the front, or, to put it simply, the secret of putting is *not putting*.

Why is driving the cart so important? Well, you may not be able to control your ball, but if you control the cart, you not only have all of your equipment and all of your opponent's equipment at your fingertips (and away from his), you also have speed, mobility, cupholders, the element of surprise, a handy source of distracting noise and movement, a large and highly maneuverable obstacle, and last, but not least, right there in the middle of the steering wheel, you have the ultimate weapon—the scorecard.

That's why, as we get ready to head for the tee, I do whatever is necessary to make sure that my bag is on the driver's side (Figure 6-3). From now on, it doesn't matter if my opponent hits his tee shot a hundred yards past my ball on all the par-4s and par-5s on the course—I'm going to "outdrive" him on every hole.

Figure 6-2. Type "B" Golfer: "Oblivious." Although possessed of formidable intellects, genuinely thick-skinned individuals such as myself are impervious to needling of any kind, or, when you get right down to it, much of anything else in the way of unsolicited input.

Figure 6-3. It's in the Bag! If someone mistakenly put your bag on the passenger side, take immediate action. If the situation permits, make the switch yourself (above) or give the bag boy a couple of bucks to do it — it's money well spent. If the cart is already up by the tee, loosen the strap on your opponent's bag, and after it falls off (above right), switch your bag to the driver's side while he retrieves it (right).

CART GOLF

We'll begin with parking strategy, or how to leave the cart in the most favorable location from your point of view, and the worst from your opponent's perspective.

The aim of these parking procedures is quite modest. You're not really trying to "hide" much more from your opponent than a little minor ball improvement, and you don't actually interfere with his swing, but all of these maneuvers produce a nice element of discomfort and frustration that keep him off balance, and they can take quite a toll when repeated during the entire round (Figure 6-4).

Now let's take a look at a somewhat more complex situation, when, as so often happens, your opponent hits his ball into the fairway, and you slice your shot deep into the woods. This seems like poor "cart management," but in fact it presents a fine opportunity for some fancy wheelwork (Figure 6-5).

If all else fails, and your impeccable driving makes no discernible dent in your opponent's machinelike play, you may need to use the cart more aggressively in a concerted effort to get the wheels to come off his game (Figure 6-6).

Figure 6-4. Basic Cart Tactics: The Angle (A); the Screen (B); and the Block (C).

A. The Angle. When you stop to hit your ball, the cart should be pointed away from the hole at about a 60-degree angle so that your opponent has to twist in his seat almost 180 degrees to watch your swing or observe the flight of the ball. Take your time with club selection. If he turns away for a moment, roll the ball over.

B. The Screen. If your balls are about the same distance from the hole, and you're both getting out to hit, leave the cart much closer to your ball in a place where it obstructs your opponent's view of your shot. This should permit you to make a small improvement in your lie as he addresses his ball.

C. The Block. When you stop to let your opponent hit, approach his ball directly from the rear and position the cart so that the front of the roof is about two feet from the furthest extent of his backswing (closer if the cart has no roof). If he asks you to move the cart, move it back about a foot, and leave the shift lever just a shade out of reverse so you can "accidentally" trigger the beeping backing-up alarm at the top of his swing. If it's a gas cart, leave it in neutral and play with the accelerator to keep it running.

102

Figure 6-5. Intermediate Cart Tactics: The Steamroller (A); the Drive-Away (B); and the Delayed Return (C).

A. The Steamroller (left). Go straight to your opponent's ball in the fairway and drive directly over it. When he points out what you've done, back over it again as you move the cart out of the way so he can hit.

B. The Drive-Away (below). As soon as he gets out of the cart, tell him he's obviously entitled to a drop and then, *before* he has had a chance to select a club, immediately drive off to look for your ball.

C. The Delayed Return. Even though you will doubtless immediately find your ball (or one very much like it) sitting up nicely in a good lie, don't hit it, and don't drive back to your opponent until you see that he has given up waiting and begun walking toward you. At this point, drive over, meeting him about halfway, and let him take a club. He's a long way from his ball, and even if he takes several, he'll probably pick the wrong ones.

Figure 6-6. Advanced Cart Tactics: The Rocket Start (A); the Brusheroo (B); and the Old Heave-Ho (C).

A. The Rocket Start. The instant your opponent is fully inside the cart, but before he is properly seated, jam on the accelerator. This is particularly effective if combined, in an unpredictable order, with the slow-as-molasses Snail Start.

B. The Brusheroo. Whenever you have to drive through overgrown or wooded areas in search of your ball (and presumably, this will be fairly often), make sure that the passenger side of the cart scrapes into any protruding branches or shrubbery. This maneuver has the additional benefit of discouraging your opponent from accompanying you on ball hunts.

C. The Old Heave-Ho. As a last resort, pick an area where there is a soft, grassy bank to the right of the cart, and then using a good solid Andretti Grip, make a sudden sharp left turn that propels your opponent out of his seat and onto the ground. Your aim isn't to put him in the hospital, but just to get him on edge, or maybe even send him completely over the edge.

"FINDING" A LOST BALL

I can see taking a penalty if you hit a ball into the middle of a water hazard (particularly if it's a second or third attempt) or if you hammer one a couple of hundred yards out of bounds and it isn't practical to play it because you'd have to cross a four-lane highway to get to where it landed. But to add a stroke to your score because you can't find a ball that decided to conceal itself in a patch of rough just off the fairway is dumb and unfair.

I've given up trying to explain to opponents that adding the childish game of hide-and-seek to the ancient sport of golf merely demeans a noble pastime, and if that's what he has in mind, why don't we go the whole hog and set up a hopscotch layout in one of the bunkers and play a round or two of jacks when we get to the green. Honestly, there's something about golf that clouds players' thinking so profoundly that you simply can't talk sense to them.

That being the case, I think the best way to handle this nonsense is to just "find" an identical ball, which if you have any sense at all is at the bottom of your pocket, or better still, already cupped lightly but securely in the palm of your hand (Figure 6-7).

If you've used Cart Golf to leave your opponent 150 yards away at the other side of the fairway, this isn't going to present much of a challenge, but for the sake of argument, let's assume he's nearby, helping you look for your ball.

If your opponent does decide to assist in the search, you have two things going for you. First, no one ever pays the slightest attention to the flight of anyone's ball except his own, so he won't be too sure where yours is, and second, an opponent will always look for your ball where he *hopes* it went, which will be the worst possible place it could have gone—usually tall grass or trees—and he's probably not going to find anything in that stuff (Figure 6-8). Needless to say, even if it really did go there, that's the last place you should ever go looking for it.

You don't want to drag out the search, because play is slow enough without making it worse, and anyway, given enough time, your opponent might actually stumble on your stupid ball in some horrible lie. Still, you have to take a minute to go through the minimum motions of searching for it in some semidecent part of the rough where you wouldn't mind finding it (Figure 6-9).

When the time comes to drop the ball (Figure 6-10), keep in mind that the release of the ball and its discovery are two separate events, coming at least ten seconds apart, and that the ball is always found *behind* you. Also, it's a small thing, but you should never have your hands in your pockets at the moment of discovery (Figure 6-11).

Figure 6-7. The Palm Hold. Always wear a white golf glove and carry the ball with a relaxed but snug grip in your gloved hand. Let your arm swing naturally as you walk.

Figure 6-8. Typical Opponent Searching for Someone Else's Ball. Let's hope your ball isn't in here, or if it is, that it picked a really good hiding place, like an abandoned ferret den about thirty feet underground. It would also be okay by me if some nasty rodent gnawed it to bits.

Figure 6-9. The Search. Choose a reasonably playable stretch of rough between your opponent and the fairway, and begin a rapid, back-and-forth, methodical-looking search, as if you had a clear idea of the general area the ball went into, give or take an acre or two.

Figure 6-10. The Release. Point to a leaf or something white that looks vaguely like a ball. Pick an awful spot, like up in the branches of a tree. As your opponent eagerly looks to see if you are indeed terminally stymied, swing your left arm back and let the ball go. Don't try to steer the ball to a perfect lie —you could end up getting "found out."

Figure 6-11. Finding the Ball. Well, looky-looky, here it is. Why, I'd almost given up hope of seeing it again. This is a very emotional moment.

"LOSING" A FOUND BALL

Just as your opponent sometimes gives you unsolicited—and unwanted—assistance in finding your ball, you may get a chance to return the favor by helping him lose his.

This is a much simpler procedure than "finding" a lost ball, and you really only need to use it in a case where your opponent's ball is sitting up in some very good lie where it's highly likely that he's going to find it.

I need hardly add that once you see it, you're going to seize the first available opportunity to step on it, but there is a right and a wrong way to "lose" a ball (Figure 6-12).

 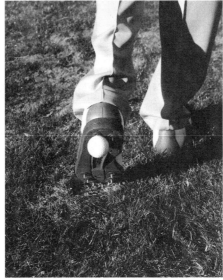

Figure 6-12. The Tromp. It takes only normal walking pressure (left) to make a ball disappear. If you try to crush the thing into the ground with the full force of your spikes, it could lead to an embarrassing result (right).

It's really on the green that the bad golfer finally comes into his own, and where, for once, even if he's playing like a monkey, he doesn't look completely ridiculous.

The putter, after all, is the one club in the bag no sane player has ever sliced a ball into the woods with, and it's the only club that after you hit with it, nobody looks at you funny when the ball only goes ten feet.

The worst putt you ever hit in your life didn't dig up a divot the size of a raccoon or sting your fingers like you stuck your mitt in a fusebox or knock some poor sucker in the gallery cold. And what gorilla have you ever played with who even once gloated because he knocked a putt a good seventy-five yards past yours?

CLUB THROWING

I think it's really lousy behavior to throw one of your clubs after a bad shot. It's also stupid. You might break it, or lose it in a hazard, and at the very least you're going to have to go get it, which can be a nuisance if it ends up in a tree.

On the other hand, an unorthodox but effective method of getting the upper hand with a hot-tempered opponent is to throw one of *his* clubs.

When he hits a terrible shot, and starts cursing a blue streak, go right over while he's still on a rampage and heartily sympathize with his anger at the flub. Get really worked up. Insist that a golfer of his caliber can hardly be expected to play decently with equipment as inferior as the miserable club that any fool could see was clearly responsible for the mishit.

While he tries to figure out what you're up to, grab the club and throw it in the woods. Shout "good riddance" as it windmills into the beyond, and assure him in a friendly sort of way that he's much better off without it.

This device is especially useful if the club in question is his putter, and you toss it in a water hazard early on in the round.

It's also comforting for the rest of us to see so many professional golfers with putting grips, stances, and strokes every bit as weird as any used by a truly bad golfer (Figure 6-13). And you can bet that not a single player on the tour goes a day without missing at least one putt that a 40-handicapper could have easily made if he hadn't picked it up.

Nevertheless, even though putting is the sole facet of the game that bad golfers have the slightest chance of mastering, that's no reason to drive yourself batty trying to sink two six-footers in a row out on the practice putting green, because no matter how easy it looks, putting is even more unpredictable than the rest of the game. If you're not careful, strokes mount up in a hurry out there on the green where everybody can see them, and you only have a minute at most to forget them before it's time to pull out the scorecard. You add together that thirty-footer that got you up by the hole, and that comebacker, and a putt you only took for practice, and a kind of backhander you sort of half hit, and the little tap-in, and all of a sudden a perfectly acceptable bogey 5 turns into a horrific triple bogey 7.

That's why I always say the only thing you can pick up from watching me putt is your ball. Now, I don't mean by that statement that if it's anywhere on the green it's automatically a gimme. There are a few putts that are in fact too long to pick up (I'd include in this category putts where you need to check to see the yardage on a nearby sprinkler head before you give the ball a roll), and there are putts you have to make because in spite of your best efforts, an opponent managed to sink his, and yours counts.

Other than that, how can you tell if a putt is a gimme? Well, I have a "rule of thumb." Reach down and place your thumb and first two fingers on the ball and exert a gentle upward pressure. If the ball comes up easily, without any need to tug at it or twist it loose, it's a gimme.

Figure 6-13. Putt for Show. The more cockeyed your putting posture, the more professional it looks. If I'm in one of those slumps where I can't sink a thing, I immediately change over to a profoundly strange putting style. That way, if the ball goes in, my opponent wonders if I'm not on to something that he ought to try (here's hoping he does), and if it doesn't, he may begin to think I'm deliberately missing to sandbag him. Neither notion will do his putting much good.

THE LAG

When you're faced with a putt too long to pick up, you have one clear objective to achieve: you must get the ball near enough to the hole to be able to mark it so your opponent will have a chance to miss his putt, and that means getting it inside your opponent's ball.

Unless his ball is right by the hole and you're a mile away, I'd try for a give-give (Figure 6-14). If he won't go along with the double-gimme, then you have no choice but to lag the ball up there and get it close. Since the last thing you want to do is leave this putt short, you want to set things up so you can give it a good solid tap (Figure 6-15).

Figure 6-14. Give-Give. If the shoe were on the other foot, I wouldn't hesitate to go along with a reciprocal concession, because these two putts are basically identical. Yes, they do differ somewhat in the minor category of sheer length, but in two other critical respects, they are identical: they both can in theory be made, and they both have been missed more times than I care to remember.

Figure 6-15. Knock It Close. Note the placement of the pin and a couple of my clubs. To the untrained eye, their placement may seem random, but they were carefully positioned to stop an overly bold putt.

THE WHAMMY

If your opponent misses his putt but still insists on continuing a foolish and potentially ruinous putting contest that's bound to cause both of your scores to snowball out of control, then so be it. Up until now, you've comported yourself with commendable restraint throughout the entire match, but this calls for extreme measures (Figure 6-16).

Figure 6-16. How to scuttle a putt: The Lean (A); The Shadow (B); the Velcro Rip (C); and the Ball from Hell (D). All are tried and true methods of putt interruption. If your opponent complains about these lighthearted interruptions, remind him pointedly that no one ever has trouble concentrating while picking up a gimme.

A. The Lean. It's a fairly simple matter to throw off your opponent's read of the green by placing yourself directly in his line and leaning imperceptibly to one side or the other as he plumb-bobs the break with his putter.

B. The Shadow. On bright, cloudless days, position yourself between the sun and the line of your opponent's putt and make bothersome shadow-producing motions with your hands and arms.

C. The Velcro Rip. If it's a putt-to-the-finish contest your opponent wants, you might as well "take off the gloves" and "throw down the gauntlet." When you "let it rip," be sure to do it very, very slowly.

D. The Ball from Hell. The instant your opponent moves his putter back, shout "Fore!" immediately throw a golf ball straight down onto the green with considerable force, and then begin looking wildly about for the source of the errant shot.

THE HOCKEY PUTT

I think it's just crazy to putt a dinky ten-footer you could make in your sleep (too bad you're awake!), but you need to know how to make this putt consistently for occasions when you're stuck playing with one of those obsessive "hole-them-all" types.

The secret of sinking these knee-knockers every time is very simple: *don't quit on the putt*. That may seem like an odd point to emphasize when you're talking about the short, soft tap required to send a ball toward the hole, but there is no other case in golf where a complete follow-through is more essential to the success of the shot (Figure 6-17).

Figure 6-17. The Hockey Putt. As you set up for this putt, keep in mind that you've got to be ready to make the goal *and* the assist. Take a stance with most of your weight on your left side, and your right foot raised and the right knee and foot turned toward the hole (A), then hit the putt, stroking it only hard enough to get it to the cup. Once you get the ball rolling (B), immediately step off on your right foot, and start walking briskly toward the hole. If the ball goes past the cup (C), redirect it with backhand "come-to-papa" raking motion while it's still moving. If it misses again, give it a final hole-out tap with the face of the putter (D). All right! (E).

THE GIMME
• •

There's a lot of confusion and uncertainty in golf as to exactly what constitutes a gimme, but I think there's general agreement that in any kind of friendly match, *some* putts—in fact, quite a few putts—should automatically be picked up without waiting for a formal notification from an opponent along the lines of "that's good" or "take it away" (Figure 6-18).

The trouble arises when a putt is not conceded, and you have to take the initiative and pick it up. This unauthorized or self-awarded gimme probably accounts for 75 percent of all picked-up putts, so it really pays to learn how to make this daring, stroke-saving move as confidently and expertly as possible (Figure 6-19).

Figure 6-18. Is It "Good"? This diagram shows the current state of thinking on gimmes. I'm grateful to the Association Internationale pour l'Etude de la Concession des Petites Frappes in Brussels for permission to incorporate the results of their latest research in this photograph.

ZONE OF CONCESSION

ZONE OF DISCUSSION

ZONE OF ACRIMONY

Figure 6-19. The "Take-Me." There are three ways to pick up an unconceded putt. The simplest—and most audacious—is to simply go over and pick the thing up (top). If your opponent loudly objects, don't "yo-yo" the ball with a series of indecisive "pick it up or put it back?" movements. Just look genuinely surprised at his stinginess, then replace the ball about halfway closer to the hole (center). At least you got a "halfie" or "demi-gimmie" out of it. A more conservative approach is to stand at the hole and rake the ball in toward your hand (bottom). This "mock putt" at least gives the appearance of an actual attempt to sink the ball, and you can sweep it up even if it goes nowhere near the cup.

THE SCORECARD

Many golfers regard the job of scorekeeping a nuisance, and they're happy to delegate it to a fellow player. I shouldn't need to tell you that if you haven't already assumed control of the scorecard by virtue of your role as driver of the cart, you should accept this responsibility with alacrity.

I'll admit that keeping track of handicaps and who's ahead in any dopey skins games, or what bet is pressed, or pleated, or whatever it is, can be a pain, but one that is nowhere near as severe as the agony of defeat. As a bad golfer, you've got to face the fact that no golf stroke, no matter how inspired, is going to let you save a 5 when you lie 6 in thick grass off the back of the green—for that you're going to need a truly inspired pencil stroke (Figure 6-20).

To properly cover the whole topic of scorekeeping, with its complex blend of behavioral psychology, higher mathematics, games theory, and hostage-negotiation tactics, would require an entire book, so I'm just going to limit myself here to the simple mechanics of entering the score in a properly ambiguous manner (Figure 6-21).

The rest is up to you—and may the best bad golfer win!

Figure 6-20. "The Little Stick." The old number 2 pencil with its short wooden shaft and space-age graphite point is your real "scoring club." I'm holding "Itsy-bitsy Bertha" with the classic Faber Grip, which is best for those delicate deletions and revisions that let you turn a 9 into a 7, or vice versa.

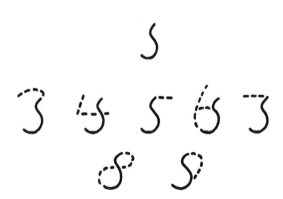

Figure 6-21. The Squiggle. This is the all-purpose easy-to-alter numerical symbol that should be used whenever possible to permit maximum flexibility in score adjustment during the round. The only one-digit number you can't create from this pencil mark is 0, but even if you're a world-class liar, I really wouldn't try to claim a hole-in-none.

CHAPTER 7

Behaving Well While Playing Badly

ETIQUETTE

I don't know whether it's because their expectations are so much lower or their charitable attitude toward Mulligans, gimmes, and minor lie improvements reflects a fundamental generosity of spirit that carries over to their fellow players, but in my experience bad golfers generally behave much better out on the course than good golfers do, particularly in the all-important matter of speed of play.

We may play badly, but we play badly *fast*. After all, if I had an 11 and you had a 12, spending time worrying about who has the "honor" on the next tee is pretty laughable, and if we're both behind trees on opposite sides of the fairway, who cares who's "away" and who throws his ball out first? Believe me, when you're a lot more likely to shoot your own weight than to shoot your age, you don't want to take all day doing it.

But even though a display of good manners is its own reward, it can pay noticeable dividends (Figure 7-1). That's why it's essential to gain a thorough appreciation of the finer points of etiquette, particularly those little displays of common courtesy and common sense that can help you knock ten to fifteen strokes—and thirty to forty-five minutes—off your next round of golf.

Figure 7-1. The Vardon Tip. The $10 you give to the starter to get him to send you out in front of the Molasses foursome tells him that you're one of those old-fashioned golfers who cares about the time-honored traditions of the game, like playing a shot at least once every minute or so and finishing the eighteenth hole without having to use a flashlight or a radioactive golf ball. Concentrate on getting good palm-to-palm contact and when you feel the bill being taken, make a smooth release.

CARE OF THE COURSE

There's nothing more annoying than trying to hit your ball out of a divot hole in the fairway or a footprint in a bunker, which would never happen if everybody did their part to get rid of as many bad lies as possible even when their balls aren't in them. That's why I always make it a habit to take good care of the course, because who knows—the golfer who benefits from my labors might just by chance turn out to be me!

In fact, I think keeping the playing environment in tip-top shape is so important, I'll repair any damage I see even *before* I hit (Figure 7-2). That way I'm sure I won't neglect to do my duty because I was overcome by sudden euphoria caused by the thrill of hitting a surprisingly good shot from what appeared at first to be a terrible lie.

Figure 7-2. Courtesy First. Don't wait until after you hit your shot to replace that divot (top) and rake that bunker smooth (bottom). If you treat it as an absolute priority as I do, and get to it right away, there's no chance you'll forget later on.

And unlike a lot of players who just yank the pin out and toss it carelessly on the green, when I get ready to putt I always go to the trouble of laying the flagstick down in a way that won't harm the putting surface (Figure 7-3). I also take very seriously my responsibility to repair ball marks on the green, even if they're not my own and not in the line of my putt. I don't care if it's an old ball mark, and it's in my opponent's line, I'll still take the time to fix it properly (Figure 7-4).

Figure 7-3. Painstaking Pin Tending. By gently placing the flagstick on the green instead of just throwing it down, I've spared the delicate grass blades a lot of wear and tear, and I've also protected the fragile edge of the hole from the buffeting that could be caused by my ball lipping out on the rim of the cup.

Figure 7-4. A Mark of Respect for the Green. To properly repair a ball mark, don't just fix the squashed down grass in the little depression caused by the impact. Help the whole affected area "breathe" by leaving the repairing tool in place for a moment or two and sticking a few tees in the surrounding turf. Remember to remove them once your opponent finishes putting.

SLOW PLAY

When one clear hole has opened up in front of the group you're playing behind, and they fail to immediately wave you through, you have to take matters into your own hands, but the niceties dictate that you should go through the motions of communicating your dissatisfaction at their pace of play prior to driving by them (Figure 7-5).

If these expressions of justifiable impatience fail to achieve their desired effect within two minutes—either because the offending players studiously ignore you or actively indicate their unwillingness to permit you to play through—you're entitled to drive ahead of them or cut across to another hole, and you may at this time elect to telegraph your disapproval directly by means of internationally recognized hand signals (Figure 7-6).

Figure 7-5. Nonverbal Appeals for Acceleration of Play. The polite method of informing a slow foursome ahead of you, but out of earshot, that they should speed up or let you by is a four-part movement.

(A) Stand with arms folded, hands under armpits, staring at the slow group (15 seconds).

125

(B) Sit cross-legged on grass and pick petals off daisy or chew grass stem (15 seconds).

(C) Stretch out on grass with one hand supporting head while other idly picks up and drops golf ball (30 seconds).

(D) Lie flat on back with both arms behind head and hat over face (45 seconds).

• • • • • • • • • •

Figure 7-6. Body French. To communicate your displeasure at an exhibition of rudeness by golfers in another playing group, extend the right arm fully with the palm facing up and the elbow slightly bent. Raise the middle finger into a vertical position, curl the tips of the remaining fingers into the palm, and press the side of the thumb against the nail of the forefinger. Raise and lower the arm once or twice with a vigorous up-and-down motion.

And finally, no book like this would be complete without some mention of the Rules of Golf (Figure 7-7).

The Rules of Golf.

Well, I guess that about wraps things up. Happy hacking, and always remember the bad golfer's credo: We don't play golf to feel bad—we play bad golf but we feel good!

Figure 7-7. The Rules of Golf. I think I would be remiss if I didn't include a copy of a complete set of the rules somewhere in this book.

SUGGESTED FURTHER READING

Leslie Nielsen's Stupid Little Golf Book, by Leslie Nielsen and Henry Beard. Doubleday, 1995. ISBN 0-385-47598-5.

Mulligan's Laws, by Henry Beard. Villard Books, 1993. ISBN 0-385-46999-3.

The Official Exceptions to the Rules of Golf, by Henry Beard. Villard Books, 1992. ISBN 0-679-40886-X.

Golfing: A Duffer's Dictionary, by Henry Beard. Workman, 1987. ISBN 0-413-63530-9.

RECOMMENDED VIEWING

Leslie Nielsen's Bad Golf Made Easier. ABC Video 45003.

Leslie Nielsen's Bad Golf My Way: How to Be Better at Being Bad. PolyGram Video 800 633 115-3.